D1196265

THE NEGRO AND THE SCHOOLS

THE NEGRO
AND
THE SCHOOLS

BY

HARRY S. ASHMORE

Foreword by

OWEN J. ROBERTS

Former Associate Justice,
Supreme Court of the United States

CHAPEL HILL

The University of North Carolina Press

Foreword

THE STUDIES UPON WHICH THIS VOLUME IS BASED HAD THEIR
inception in a series of conferences held by the Fund for the
Advancement of Education in the course of its normal business of seeking out educational areas which might benefit
from an infusion of Ford Foundation money. The Fund soon
came, as had many a philanthropy before it, to the peculiar
problems involved in the schooling of the American Negro.
And there, in the late spring and early summer of 1953, the
Fund's officers found unanimous agreement among the educators they consulted—white and Negro, Southern and non-
Southern—that there was an urgent need for a new and
comprehensive look at the structure of bi-racial education in
the United States.

The need has existed for a long time but is more pressing
now than ever. States and communities where segregated
schools were long the rule have in recent years been making
important adjustments toward equalizing educational opportunities and in some cases toward integrating children of
different races. This complex process of adjustment has had
its reflection in the budget and policy debates of legislatures,
in the deliberations of local school boards, and in a long line
of cases before the courts. The most recent and perhaps most

publicized of such cases were pending before the United States Supreme Court when this research project began. Whatever their outcome, it seemed likely that the courts of the land would continue to play an important role in this adjustment process. The final burden and responsibility for our schools rests, however, upon the local citizens who operate and support them. These people need and deserve all the help they can get, and one of their greatest needs is for objective facts which will guide them toward wise decisions in the face of difficult problems. It was primarily with the needs of these practical "decision-makers" in the field of education in view that the directors and officers of the Fund for the Advancement of Education decided to support the present study.

At the outset this statement of principle was adopted:

1. The Fund will not undertake to argue the case for or against segregation in public education, and in no sense will it become involved as an advocate on either side of the issues now pending before the Supreme Court.

2. Aside from the possible consequences of this litigation, there is a need for an objective re-appraisal of the bi-racial aspects of our educational system. This should take into account the great shifting of population in recent years, the rapidly improving economic status of the region most affected, as well as any significant changes in prevailing attitudes and practices.

3. Since no single institution or agency is equipped to handle such a study within the time limitation involved, the Fund will bring together a temporary research staff consisting of persons who are specially qualified to examine the various aspects of the educational structure. . . .

The undertaking of research on such a scale directly under the aegis of the Fund is an unorthodox procedure for this or any other foundation. Yet it had the great advantage of drawing upon the experience and talents of men and women who had spent many years in the study of various aspects of this complex area of human relationships. Perhaps in no other way could such a body of research have been pooled in such a relatively short time.

This volume, then, is a summary and interpretation of the findings of the more than forty scholars who labored at one time or another in what came to be called the Ashmore Project. It will be followed by three additional works to be published by the University of North Carolina Press which will present in greater detail the basic material thus gathered. These are: an essentially sociological work based upon field studies of communities in transition from segregation to integration in the public schools, to be edited by Professor Robin Williams of Cornell University; a collection of field studies of Southern institutions of higher education which have lately admitted Negroes, to be edited by Professor Guy B. Johnson of the University of North Carolina; and a composite of the public school administration, population, and economic studies to be jointly edited by Mr. Philip Hammer, who served the project as research director, and Professors Truman Pierce of George Peabody College for Teachers, John Maclachlan of the University of Florida, and Ernst Swanson of Emory University. In addition, much of the basic legal research undertaken for the project by Dean Robert A. Leflar and Professor Wylie H. Davis of the University of Arkansas Law School already has been published in the *Harvard Law Review.*

This volume and those that follow it are intended to bring into focus the dimensions and the nature of a complex educational problem that in many ways provides a significant test of American democracy. The ultimate solution of that problem will rest with the men and women who make and execute public school policy in thousands of local school districts, and their actions will be conditioned by the degree of understanding of the general public which supports their efforts with its tax dollars. If this project serves to assist them in their task the Fund for the Advancement of Education will feel that it has wisely invested a portion of the risk capital of American education with which it is entrusted.

My colleagues join me in thanking Mr. Harry Ashmore for his wise direction of the project and his skillful preparation of this report. We wish also to express our gratitude to Mr. Philip Hammer and his fellow researchers for their tireless and competent efforts.

OWEN J. ROBERTS

Philadelphia, Pennsylvania

Contents

PART TWO

The Figures Tell the Story

I. Schools: Tables

II. Population: Tables

CONTENTS

PART THREE

Appendices

Charts

Introduction

IT WOULD SEEM TO BE A SIMPLE TASK TO TAKE THE OUTSIDE
dimensions of the dual public school system which has
served whites and Negroes in the United States through all
our history, and not much more difficult to appraise its general effects upon public education.

In practice, however, this has turned out to be an enor-
mously complex assignment, one that has taxed the skills of
the scholars who performed the necessary hard labor and
often perplexed the newspaper editor who came finally to
write this summary report of their findings.

In the first place—and for several reasons this is an important consideration to bear in mind—the structure of public
education in the United States is almost as decentralized
as the nation's system of municipal government. National
and state agencies set its standards, or attempt to, but final
administrative authority is vested in thousands of local school
districts and exercised by hundreds of thousands of elected
school board members and appointed officials. There is wide
variety in the methods by which these agencies keep their
accounts and, although formalized reports on their activities
drift upward through fixed channels, there are no absolutes

by which they can be measured or compared from state to state.

Moreover, these official data are usually concerned with things as they are, while this study is also concerned with things as they may be in the wake of the legal and extra-legal pressures against segregation which have their current focus in the dual school system. This of necessity projects this volume well beyond the safe bounds of public school and census records and into an area of violently conflicting opinions and prejudices. Here objectivity (assuming that mere mortals can achieve it) provides no immunity against the advocates who for more than a generation have been engaged in a great debate on racial segregation. Change must be the central theme in any appraisal that touches upon the relationships between the majority and minority races—but the mere recording of change can be controversial when emotions cancel out the laws of logic.

This is one of the natural hazards of a work of this kind. There are others—including the persistent temptation to stray off down one of the inviting side roads that open up in the consideration of the past, present, and future of bi-racial education. This could be avoided only by holding fast to the criterion that nothing would be included here that did not bear directly upon public education in the United States. Thus a great deal of history, and much contemporary sociological matter, has been drastically compressed and drawn in with broad strokes that cannot do justice to the finer shadings of scholarly interpretation and qualification.

My own role in this undertaking changed significantly while the work was in progress. I began with the assumption that I would serve simply as an editor; in the end I found myself operating as a reporter—performing the essentially journalistic function of briefing the mass of research data and fitting it, as best I could, into the larger context of the developing pattern of American race relations. Thus the scholars deserve credit for the salient facts that have gone into this report, while any blame that may attach to the speculations and value judgments belongs to me.

In many important ways this volume puts to the test one of my cherished theories—that in addition to its usual functions of preparing a first draft of history, entertaining children of all ages, and promoting the sale of certain goods and services, journalism should serve as a two-way bridge between the world of ideas and the world of men. In any event my experience as a journalist in a company of scholars has strengthened my conviction that no problems are beyond resolution by reasonable men—not even the thorny ones that lie in the uncertain area between the polar attitudes of the American white, who does not yet accept the Negro as his equal, and the American Negro, who is no longer satisfied with anything less.

Little Rock, Arkansas   Harry S. Ashmore

PART ONE

*Bi-Racial Education
in the United States*

1 LEGAL STATUS OF SEGREGATION IN THE PUBLIC SCHOOLS

Segregation required ; *17 states and District of Columbia*

Segregation permitted in varying degrees *4 states*

Segregation prohibited *16 states*

No specific legislation on segregation *11 states*

CHAPTER ONE

The Genesis of Bi-Racial Education

MORE THAN A CENTURY AGO THE FIRST LEGAL ATTACK UPON segregation in the public schools of the United States was initiated in Boston. It was a singular case in many ways. In terms of the mass of American Negroes, who were still held in bondage in the Southern states and denied access to an education of any kind, it was a magnificent irrelevancy. Even to the handful of freedmen who lived outside the South the lawsuit could hardly have seemed a matter of great moment. Nevertheless, the issue was drawn and argued with great moral fervor, for it was pressed as an article of faith by the hardy band of New England abolitionists who were already launched upon the course which was to shape so much of the nation's history.

The lawyer of record in the first school segregation case was Charles Sumner himself—the brilliant, contentious Yankee who was to be enshrined in the North as the era's most militant crusader for Negro rights and reviled in the South as an arch-villain of Reconstruction. Sumner appeared on behalf of a Negro girl who had been barred from a white school under a local ordinance providing for separate education of the races. There was no Fourteenth Amendment for the Court to interpret, but Sumner's arguments in *Roberts* v.

City of Boston were not substantially different from those that were to be heard in state and federal courts a hundred years later.

The bill of rights of the Massachusetts constitution, he contended, forbade any legal distinctions based on race when it proclaimed all citizens to be born equal. The operation of segregated public schools, Sumner argued, "tends to deepen and to perpetuate the odious distinction of caste, founded in a deep-rooted prejudice in public opinion." And finally he sought to show that the separate schools of Boston were not in fact equal, pointing out that his client had to walk 2,100 feet to attend her classes, while a white school was only 800 feet from her door.

The Massachusetts Supreme Court held against Sumner and handed down a decision that also was to have its echoes a century later. Chief Justice Shaw found that segregation of the races did not in itself constitute discrimination, and held that when the Boston School Committee provided substantially equal schools for Negroes it had reasonably exercised local powers not specifically denied it by higher authority. And Chief Justice Shaw dismissed Sumner's central thesis with the opinion that any caste distinction aggravated by segregated schools, "if it exists, is not created by law and probably cannot be changed by law."

The decision in the *Roberts* case came down in 1849, but it served as only a minor deterrent to the abolitionists. Clothed, as they were by their own definition, in the armor of the Lord, they shifted their attack to the political arena, and by 1855 they had mobilized sufficient public opinion to persuade the Massachusetts legislature to repudiate the Court. In that year segregation in the public schools of the state was specifically prohibited by statute.

Sumner himself must have looked upon the *Roberts* case as only a minor skirmish on the periphery of the great struggle in which he was rapidly assuming leadership. Yet the issue drawn before the Court had great symbolic importance, for it demonstrated that those who spoke so passionately on behalf of the abolition of slavery sought not merely to remove the black man's chains but to admit him forthwith at every level of society as a matter of moral right. Certainly it helped firm the resolve of the South, which had closed ranks under the injunction of John C. Calhoun, who, with the support of many Southern divines, had also donned the Lord's armor and proclaimed slavery a positive good. Calhoun's doctrine of state's rights would sound across the years too, whenever the issue of segregation arose in the South:

Our fate as a people is bound up in the question. If we yield we will be extirpated; but if we successfully resist we will be the greatest and most flourishing people of modern time. It is the best substratum of population in the world; and one on which great and flourishing commonwealths can be most easily and safely reared. . . .

The door must be closed against all interference on the part of the general government in any form, whether in the District of Columbia, or in the states and territories. The highest grounds are the safest.

As it turned out, neither side was able to hold to the high ground for long. As the great debate over slavery thundered a prelude to civil war, Sumner fought doggedly in the Senate against compromise. When a middle-of-the-roader chided him for "forgetting the other side," he shouted, "There is no other side!" His contemporaries from the South felt the same, and the debate could only be terminated by the sound of guns at Fort Sumter.

Four years of the bloodiest warfare the nation has known settled the issue of slavery, but it did not resolve the concurrent questions of full citizenship for the emancipated slaves. Let it be said for Sumner and his colleagues that this was no fault of theirs. They denounced the mild Reconstruction policies of Abraham Lincoln; they came within a single vote of impeaching Andrew Johnson when he adopted them; and they feuded bitterly with the phlegmatic Ulysses Grant from the day he took office. In the course of these battles Sumner assiduously kept the issue of segregation in education alive. In 1873 he sponsored a bill which specifically banned the practice, and after Sumner's death in 1874 the measure was enacted in the Senate. An opposing minority, presumably pro-segregation, kept the measure from coming to a vote in the House. But when the House Judiciary Committee reported an amended civil rights bill containing a provision expressly permitting "separate but equal" schools a presumably anti-segregation minority managed to keep it off the floor. The final compromise in the Civil Rights Act of 1875 was the omission of all reference to the schools in the measure which was intended to implement the Fourteenth Amendment.

As a practical matter, the public school issue was raised and dismissed in a vacuum—for at the end of the Civil War the South had little in the way of a public school system to which the Negro could have been admitted even if the Congress had so willed.

Unlike the rest of the nation, and despite the prodding of Southern leaders like Thomas Jefferson, the ante-bellum South had shown little interest in universal education. Well-born Southern whites were instructed by tutors or attended private academies; most others remained unlettered unless, like Abraham Lincoln in his Kentucky cabin, they pursued learning on their own. In 1866 there was no effective state system of public education anywhere in the region, and only a few of the larger cities maintained "free schools." There was no schooling at all for Negroes; indeed, in several of the

Southern states teaching slaves to read and write was officially a crime.

The end of the Civil War brought to the South two years
of comparatively gentle "presidential Reconstruction," followed by a decade of stringent "congressional Reconstruction" in which the region was divided into five military districts and federal occupation troops were given the mission
of enforcing the Fourteenth Amendment and the new statutes
relating to Negro suffrage. Under the federal guns state
governments were established by a coalition of "carpet-
bagger" Yankees newly come South, "scalawag" white Southerners who allied themselves with the triumphant Republican party, and newly-enfranchised Negroes. One of the first
objectives of these Reconstruction governments was to establish systems of public education, and for their support they
levied the first universal school taxes the region had known.
Yet, remarkably enough, only three of the states seriously
attempted to launch the new schools on a non-segregated
basis. In South Carolina "mixed" schools were established at
Columbia and Charleston, but they survived only briefly and
the closest the races came to mixing was while attending
classes in separate rooms of the same buildings. In Louisiana
a ban on segregation was written into the constitution of
1868, but in his history of Negro education Horace Mann
Bond reports that he could find only one recorded instance
in which the provision was invoked. The children of P.B.S.
Pinchbeck, Louisiana's Negro lieutenant-governor under the
Reconstruction government, attempted to enroll in the boy's
high school in New Orleans, only to be driven out by a mob
of white students. One of the leaders of the mob later offered
an explanation which can serve as an epitaph for the whole
movement: "They were good enough Niggers, but they were
still Niggers. . . ."

Most of the Reconstruction governments made no real

effort to integrate the new public schools, and while they adopted policies of financial support that were theoretically even-handed, the results were usually prejudicial to the Negro wing of the emerging dual system. Some followed the lead of Kentucky, which levied a tax of two mills on real property for school support, plus a fifty-cent poll tax on males with children of school age—but provided that the Negro schools should receive only the taxes paid by Negroes.

There can be no doubt that the emancipated slaves ardently desired schooling; education was looked upon as one of the marks of their new status. Yet in the list of the freedmen's immediate needs, education came a poor second to the pressing economic problems facing a people who owned no land and for the most part were trained only in agricultural skills. Bond noted that in South Carolina, Mississippi, and Louisiana "the mixed-school issue was put forward by white idealists who believed that the separate school was undemocratic." And he added in his summary of the Reconstruction period:

Those who argued against mixed schools were right in believing that such a system was impossible in the South, but they were wrong in believing that the South could, or would, maintain equal schools for both races. Those who argued for mixed schools were right in believing that separate schools meant discrimination against Negroes, but they were opposed to the logic of history and the reality of human nature and racial prejudices.

Under the circumstances, Negro education during the Reconstruction period inevitably came to be regarded as more a function of the federal government and of private philanthropy than as a local responsibility—which none of the ruined Southern states was in position to discharge anyway. The Freedmen's Bureau, set up by Congress in 1865, launched more than 4,000 elementary schools serving a quarter of a million people, and since the bureau was concerned solely with assisting Negroes, these were perforce segregated schools. Important private assistance came from Northern church and benevolent organizations which sent not only funds but missionaries into the region to aid the cause of Negro education. In the turbulent post-war era, as Jonathan Daniels has remarked, a newcomer from the North was as likely to bear a carpetbag packed with a Bible, a primer, and six bars of sweet-scented soap as one containing a derringer, a deck of cards, and a quart of rye whiskey.

Reconstruction, with its high-riding Negro hopes and its white despair, its occupation troops and its missionaries, its political chaos and its economic privation, lasted for varying periods in the Southern states, but it was over in all of them by 1877 when the last Federal troops were withdrawn. Out of that unsettled era emerged the rudiments of the public education system which still serves the South, and the traditions that have kept it segregated through the years. The principle of universal education written into the Reconstruction constitutions survived when the Southern whites returned to power, but everywhere the laws were changed to provide that the two races were to be educated separately. The very survival of the concept of equal educational opportunity in the face of the violent white reaction to Reconstruction has been found worthy of comment by most of those who have studied the period. In the decades that followed the Negro was to be effectively stripped of his franchise, and thereby of his only means of enforcing his demand for free public education, while at the same time the North by tacit agreement abandoned its role of militant enforcer of Negro rights. Thus, a decade after it had lost the war, the white Southern leadership was again in power, and again, with only abstract limitations, free to define racial relationships as it saw fit. Yet the Southern commitment to educate the

Negro as well as the white child, although it would long be imperfectly fulfilled, was never formally renounced—and, indeed, has seldom been officially challenged.

If the South did little to provide an education for Negroes in those post-war years, it did little more for the whites. There were, of course, compelling practical reasons for its failure. The stricken region was entirely bypassed by the industrial revolution which was transforming the face of America and creating great concentrations of wealth in the North and in the newly-opened West. The South remained an agricultural province, and a conquered one, and poverty was almost universal. There simply was no economic base upon which to build an adequate system of public schools where none had existed before.

Its bi-racial character was only incidental to the slow and painful growth of public education in the South. By 1900, only one Southern state—Kentucky—had made school attendance compulsory. Less than 40 per cent of the children of school age in the region attended school regularly, and of these only one in ten reached the fifth grade. Over 11 per cent of the whites and 48 per cent of the Negroes lacked even the rudiments of reading and writing. The great drive for public education, which was to draw much of its strength from the political rebellion of the "poor whites" against the "Bourbons," was yet to come.

While the wall of segregation was being mortared tight in the South, a similar if less dramatic process was going on almost everywhere else in the nation in the post-Civil War years. Negroes were still few in the non-South, and they generally enjoyed the right of franchise. But the religious fervor of the abolitionist era was fading, to be replaced by a prevailing conservatism in racial matters. Wherever Negroes concentrated in sizable numbers they ran into social and economic pressures which forced them to live apart from the white community, and sometimes this *de facto* segregation was bolstered by law.

In this period the legal doctrine enunciated by Chief Justice Shaw in *Roberts* v. *City of Boston,* although it had been set aside by statute in his own state, came to provide a pattern-setting precedent in the courts of the non-South. State-enforced segregation was upheld successively in Ohio, Indiana, California, New York, West Virginia, and Missouri. The Fourteenth Amendment was disposed of by the same line of reasoning applied to the Massachusetts bill of rights in the *Roberts* case.

It was perhaps symptomatic of the declining popular interest in the Negro cause that none of this litigation reached the United States Supreme Court. But in 1896, in the famous *Plessy* v. *Ferguson* case, the Court dragged Justice Shaw's precedent into federal jurisprudence by a side door. The case at issue involved an attack upon a Louisiana statute requiring separation of the races on trains traveling within the state. Plessy, a man of one-eighth Negro descent, asked the Court to invalidate the Louisiana law as violative of his personal rights under the Thirteenth and Fourteenth Amendments. The Court, with Mr. Justice Harlan vigorously dissenting, refused:

Laws permitting, and even requiring [separation of the races] in places where they are liable to be brought into contact do not necessarily imply the inferiority of either race to the other, and have been generally, if not universally, recognized as within the competency of the state legislatures in the exercise of their police power. The most common instance of this is connected with the establishment of separate schools for white and colored children, which has been held a valid exercise of the legislative power even by courts of states where the political rights of the colored race have been longest and most earnestly enforced.

Thus the "separate but equal" doctrine in education was given the sanction of federal law by virtue of a *dictum*, or side remark of the Court. Actually, this circumstance may have given the precedent even greater strength, for here the Court went out of its way to recognize that segregation in education was a general American practice, not a uniquely Southern one. In any event, the Court had firmly imbedded the durable doctrine which has been the determinant in all subsequent litigation involving the dual school system.

CHAPTER TWO

The New South and the Era of Booker T. Washington

POWERFUL FORCES FOR CHANGE WERE STIRRING IN THE SOUTH *
as the nation rounded the turn into the Twentieth Century.
The industrial revolution was belatedly dotting the Piedmont
country with textile mills, raising steel plants in the ore-rich
hills of Alabama, and rimming the Southern cities with light
industries. In Atlanta a prophet had arisen to proclaim a New
South, and by 1886 Henry Grady was taking his message to
the former enemy. "Will [you] permit the prejudice of war
to remain in the hearts of the conquerors, when it has died
in the hearts of the conquered?" he demanded of the New
England Society in New York. And to the Boston Merchants
Association he said: "We need not go one step further unless
you concede right here that the people I speak for are just
as honest, as sensible and as just as your people." The Georgia
editor was cheered wherever he went, and on the rhetorical
level the War Between the States was finally over.

In the Southern political arena a great internal struggle
marked the closing years of the old century. In the dark hours

---

* Throughout this report the South, unless otherwise specifically indentified,
refers to Virginia, North Carolina, South Carolina, Georgia, Florida, Tennessee, Alabama, Mississippi, Louisiana, Arkansas, Texas, Kentucky, and
Oklahoma.

of Reconstruction the white South had naturally turned to its wartime leaders—the distinguished old soldiers who had written on the battlefields the only glorious chapters in the brief history of the Confederacy. In South Carolina, General Wade Hampton was called forth to ride at the head of the Red Shirts and break the carpetbag rule; in Tennessee the great Nathan Bedford Forrest wore the robes of the Grand Dragon of the Ku Klux Klan. When the Reconstruction governments and their "black and tan legislatures" were broken and swept away, political power naturally fell again to the old "Bourbons," and they exercised it as they always had—cautiously, conservatively, and with little apparent understanding of the tragic realities that beset their constituents.

Revolt was not long in coming. The gallant past that seemed to sustain the political orators was less important to the back-country farmers than the bleak present. Soon they were referring to the late unpleasantness as "a rich man's war and a poor man's fight." In South Carolina a vitriolic, one-eyed curmudgeon called Pitchfork Ben Tillman arose in the upcountry to take out after the patriarchal Hampton, and in a decade Tillman had control of the state government and was on his way to founding a crude and vigorous political dynasty. Tom Watson rallied a fanatical following along the muddy back roads of Georgia. All across the region the Populist banner was broken out, and an era of factional infighting began which was to produce some of the South's most notorious demagogues and some of its most enduring political reforms.

This was an agrarian revolt, and its rank and file were referred to contemptuously as the "red necks" and the "wool hat boys." But one of its first and most insistent demands was for more and better state-financed education—for free common schools and for vocational schools and colleges that could equip the rising generation to grapple with the grinding economic problems that beset the South.

This political process had little positive meaning for the Southern Negro, who by 1900 had lapsed into the long twilight period which would continue until the New Deal years —the period when he was no longer a slave and not yet a citizen. His vote became a prize in the struggle between the bitterly contending white leaders, but in the end they were to unite in the successful effort to strip him of his franchise.

Negroes sat in at the formation of some of the state Populist parties, and Charles B. Spahr, a Northern scholar, wrote of the year 1894: "The color line seemed to have broken down and the time seemed near at hand when all the political rights of the Negro, and all the rights that could be secured to him through political action, would be granted him." A closer look, however, reveals that few, if any, of the whites who sought Negro political support compromised their basic belief in the principles of white supremacy.

From the beginning the Bourbons, who retained control of the Democratic party, fought the Populists with every means at hand and the elections of 1892 were marked by wholesale fraud, vote-buying and election-stealing—in the course of which the Democrats managed to deliver a substantial number of Negro votes to their candidates.

In desperation some of the state Populist parties in 1894 turned to fusion with the Republicans—although some Populist leaders, including Tom Watson of Georgia, denounced the movement as a departure from principle. The Negro vote was a primary issue, with the proponents of fusion insisting that it was necessary to protect the Negro against "coercion and fraud" by the Democrats. In North Carolina, where the Populists entered into a formal coalition with the Republicans, Southern Populism reached its peak in 1894. The coalition elected both United States senators and five congressmen, and captured control of the North Carolina legislature. Over 1,000 Negroes held public office in the South briefly during this period—a circumstance leading, as one historian has succinctly put it, to riots.

Toward the end of the nineties there was widespread public revulsion against the tumultuous and corrupt political practices that had marked the agrarian revolt, and the efforts of the Bourbons to put it down. In 1890, Mississippi, where the Populists had had little truck with the Negroes, put through the "Mississippi Plan" for their final disfranchisement. A decade later similar legislation was universal throughout the South, and many of the old Populist leaders— Tom Watson of Georgia was a notable example—were waving the banners of white supremacy even more vigorously than their Bourbon enemies. An ironic by-product of the movement was that some of the devices for disfranchising the Negro—based primarily on property and literacy qualifications and poll taxes—also had the effect of stripping many poor whites of the ballot.

In the three decades during which he precariously held his franchise, the Negro was more a pawn than a participant in the main stream of Southern politics. So it was with the economic currents that began to change the face of the South; they too swept past the Negro, leaving him isolated in his ordained role of tenant farmer, common laborer, and domestic servant—"the drawer of water and hewer of wood." The new cotton mills drew their hands from among the white farmers of the hill country, and their company towns were citadels of segregation from their inception. The small, diversified factories that sprang up during the period made no place for the Negro at their machines.

Under these circumstances, the Negro could only be a passive partner in the new drive for public education. He was never effectively represented in the halls where school budgets were drawn up, and he paid little of the taxes that sustained them.

In the early years of the century public education in the South received significant impetus from the outside through the contributions of such philanthropists as Rockefeller and Peabody. Within the meager limits of their financial ability, the Southern states matched these private grants with public funds, and by the end of World War I every state had a compulsory school law, and enough schools to give the law meaning.

Negro education shared in this general movement, but it was also the object of direct Northern philanthropies shaped to its special needs. The Anna T. Jeanes Fund in 1908 inaugurated the "Jeanes Teacher" program, financing Negro supervisors to improve the quality of instruction in rural schools. Beginning in 1913, the Julius Rosenwald Fund provided grants for Negro school construction, and by 1932 more than 5,000 Negro school buildings in 883 counties of 15 Southern and border states had been built with Rosenwald aid—about one-fifth of all the Negro schools in 12 of the states. A breakdown of the total cost of these buildings provides a fair indication of the sources of the effort behind Negro education in the period. Although the Rosenwald grants provided an invaluable incentive they accounted for only about 15 per cent of the money spent on the program; about 64 per cent came from public funds, 4 per cent from sympathetic Southern whites, and 17 per cent from direct contributions made by Negroes themselves.

By any measurement, however, the Negro branch of the dual school system lagged far behind. At the end of the Rosenwald building program, the per-pupil value of Negro school property was less than one-fifth as great as that of white schools. An even more telling index to the relative growth of the dual school systems is provided by a comparison of teachers' salaries. Between 1900 and 1930, the average white salary rose from slightly less than $200 to $900, while the average Negro salary rose from $100 to $400. And these figures reflect the peak of a national boom, both in national income and in school population.

Could this disparate treatment, then, be said to conform to the Supreme Court's *Plessy* doctrine of equality as the corollary of segregation in the public schools? As a practical matter, so far as the South was concerned, it could. "Separate but equal" was written into the declared educational policy of all the Southern states, but there is nothing to indicate that the men who wrote it expected the doctrine to have the literal meaning it would attain 50 years later. Rather, the policy provided a verbal escape from a situation which most Southern whites regarded as insoluble. Through it, the Southern states declared their determination to maintain segregation; the ideal of equal opportunity was secondary, a goal to be seriously considered only after the educational needs of the whites had been met.

The Negro wing of the dual school system operated from the beginning under the same administrative structure as the white wing, but in the early days most school officials gave little attention to their Negro charges. They reflected the attitude of the great majority of whites who believed that Negroes needed no more than the bare essentials of grade school education to assume their proper place in the social order, and, no matter what the statutes might show for the record, this became the settled policy in the region. It is symptomatic that the first state directors of Negro education in the South, all of them whites, received all or part of their salaries from private philanthropists. The few educators who gave serious thought to education of a more advanced nature for Negroes usually justified it with the "industrial" label popularized by the great Negro leader of the period, Booker T. Washington of Tuskegee. There was an ironic overtone in this, since the New South's industries showed no signs of making room for Negroes above the level of common labor. But the greatest handicap was the practical fact that vocational education is more costly than the "classical" variety, which under the slender school budgets of the time made the label virtually meaningless.

Thus most Negro children received the same *kind* of education as the whites, inferior as it may have been in quantity and quality. And this in itself was something of a violation of the spirit of the prevailing public policy, for it was hardly logical to teach the equalitarian lessons of American history and the duties and responsibilities of citizenship to a people who were presumed to be permanently relegated to the lower orders.

The effects of this unwritten policy were evident in the concentration of Negro children in the lower grades during the early years of the century. As late as 1920, 85 per cent of all Negro pupils in the South were enrolled in the first four grades. In 1916, there were only 67 Negro public high schools, with fewer than 20,000 students.

For the Southern Negro segregation came with the first schools he knew, and this was hardly a matter of separate concern since he lived in a wholly segregated society. He might dream the old dream of full equality, but his immediate goal was to get a school, any kind of school, and then to improve it—and that seemed task enough for one lifetime.

In retrospect, many of the militant Negro leaders who arose in the twenties and thirties have condemned their race's spokesmen of the post-Reconstruction era as overly conservative, and have applied the contemptuous term "Uncle Tom" to those who urged a conciliatory approach to the dominant whites. The eloquent and frequently bitter W. E. B. DuBois wrote in *Black Reconstruction:*

Their own leaders decried "politics" and preached submission. All their efforts toward manly self-assertion were distracted by defeatism and counsels of despair, backed by the powerful propaganda of a religion which taught meekness, sacrifice and humility.

Yet there was significant progress in the period which was symbolized by the statesmanship of Booker T. Washington, whose life spanned the era from slavery to World War I. Washington's only weapons were polite persuasion and the exemplary record of his own remarkable career. He could appeal to the sense of justice of the white man, and, in an echo of Henry Grady's economic theme, to his self-interest when he reminded him that he could not keep the Negro in the ditch without staying down with him. Washington carefully phrased his arguments for the advancement of Negro education so as to avoid any suggestion of an attack upon the ramparts of segregation; his symbol of the South was his supplicating hand, and he reminded his white audiences that the region could advance with the races remaining as separate as his spread fingers "in all things that are purely social."

Washington was pleading his race's case at a time when the violence of Reconstruction was still a green memory. In no other way could he have rallied the powerful white support that came to him in the wake of such approving comment as Clark Howell's in the *Atlanta Constitution:* "The whole [1895 Atlanta Exposition] speech is a platform upon which the whites and blacks can stand with full justice to each race."

A few months before he died in 1915, Washington expressed personal opposition to segregation laws as unjust, unnecessary, and tending to harm both races in the long run. But it was his moderate philosophy of the earlier years that generally prevailed in the South until the thirties. It provided a refuge for Negroes, and for responsible Southern whites, when a revived and debased Ku Klux Klan rode over the region in the twenties and the uninhibited political heirs of the old Populists professed to see new threats to white supremacy on every side.

The Klan in this reincarnation was not solely a Southern phenomenon; the movement, which now listed Jews and Catholics among its targets as well as Negroes, spread over much of the United States and became a prime symbol of the nation's post-World War I reaction. A contributing factor was the great out-migration of Southern Negroes in the war years and after, which changed both the complexion of the cities of the North, and their complacent attitudes. Between 1920 and 1930, the Negro population of the non-South increased by one million, or more than 50 per cent. In the wake of the great influx of Southern Negroes came new problems for the nation's great cities, and in many instances they were met by old solutions. Charles S. Johnson, the distinguished Negro sociologist, thus described the result:

Following the migration of large numbers of Negroes from the poorer schools of the South to the northern centers there was noted an increasing tendency to group them separately. Some of the school authorities complained that the serious retardation of the Southern children constituted sufficient warrant for separate treatment.... With increased numbers of Negroes in the Northern cities the tendency to segregation increases, and this tendency is viewed with apprehension by many Negroes....

Yet, although there were palpable inequalities in the dual schools of the South, and mounting concern among Negroes over the tendency toward segregation in the non-South, the Negro leadership did not turn to the courts until the thirties.

Many Southern Negroes apparently felt that legal action would endanger the delicate balance of their relationship with the dominant whites, while the Northern Negro leadership saw no hope of relief under the doctrine of *Plessy*.

Whatever the reason, between 1896, when the *Plessy* decision was handed down, and 1930, only three cases involving Negro education came before the Supreme Court. In none of these was school segregation directly challenged, nor did the Court find occasion to order relief of any kind for Negro plaintiffs.

In 1899 the Supreme Court heard an appeal by a group of Augusta, Georgia, Negroes who demanded an end to public support for two white high schools after the sole Negro high school had been discontinued. The majority opinion in *Cumming* v. *Richmond County* held that the relief requested was improper, specifically pointing out that the issue of race separation was not before the Court.

In 1908 the Court heard the case of *Berea College* v. *Kentucky*, which turned upon the right of a privately chartered college to teach both races in defiance of the Kentucky law making segregation mandatory. The Court ruled against Berea on technical grounds, but the case was generally accepted as a reflection of the Court's feeling that segregation was a matter better left to the states.

Gong Lum v. *Rice*, which went up from Mississippi in 1927, only served to emphasize one of the odd aspects of segregation. The issue here was whether Mississippi could properly classify a Chinese child as "colored" and therefore require her to attend a Negro school. While the Court upheld the Mississippi law, Chief Justice Taft took the occasion to offer a reminder that the "separate but equal" doctrine was still around: "Had the petition alleged specifically that there was no colored school in Martha Lum's neighborhood to which she could conveniently go, a different question would have been presented. . . ."

None of these cases directly challenged the constitutionality of segregation in education. The historic legal battles which would bring the Court to re-examine its previous interpretation of the Fourteenth Amendment still lay ahead in the period when the shock of the great depression marked the beginning of a new era in race relations.

CHAPTER THREE

The Depression Years: Crisis and Change

IN THE THIRTIES HENRY GRADY'S NEW SOUTH RAN HEAD-ON into the Great Depression. The paralysis of credit and the disappearance of risk capital cut off the roots of expansion in the still underdeveloped region. The new factories which were the symbol of the South's re-birth began to shut down, and collapsing farm prices shattered the still-dominant agrarian economy. Along the back roads baled cotton stood under the chinaberry trees, waiting for the market to rise, and from Virginia to Texas white men and black sang a mournful refrain:

> Ten cent cotton and forty cent meat,
> How in hell can a poor man eat?

By the time the advisors of Franklin Roosevelt got around to formally designating the South as the Nation's Number One Economic Problem not even the most sensitive Chamber of Commerce secretary could quibble with the verdict. The depression had turned the calendar back to the seventies and most Southerners were again grappling with the elementary problems of survival. The high priority public education had begun to attain was lost; under the pressures of privation the schools slid back down the scale.

The public school system of the South was still far short of meeting the growing demand for education when public funds shrank below the peril point. Further expansion was out of the question at a time when it took all the most dedicated officials could do to keep the existing schools open. And many failed even that minimum task; school terms were cut back on a wholesale scale and many discouraged teachers received their pay in heavily-discounted scrip.

The South's school problems, while not different in kind from those that faced school systems everywhere in the depression-ridden nation, were accentuated by the region's late start in the field of public education and its historic lack of resources. On top of all that, the South was faced with a population boom which coincided with economic collapse. Southern school attendance hit its pre-World War II peak in the bleak year of 1934; the 700,000 increase in attendance in the region during the thirties was equivalent to 90 per cent of the nation's total gain. For the first time since the turn of the century, the population of the South grew faster than that of the rest of the nation. The region's birthrate dropped off from the preceding decade, but it remained higher than the national average. And now the depression had cut back the great out-migration that had sent 1.3 million Southerners to the industrial cities of the non-South during the decade after World War I. Only a half million would follow them during the thirties, and most of these would migrate toward the end of the decade when employment opportunities again began to exert their magnetic attraction. The South's population gain for the period was about 3.3 million, or nearly 10 per cent, as compared with 6 per cent for the rest of the nation.

The slowing of out-migration, which had been preponderantly Negro, meant a gain in the proportion of the nation's Negro population living in the South. The 465,000 increase in the region's minority group was greater than that of the preceding decade, while the Negro population in the rest of the country increased only by about half. And even though this "backing up" of Negro population in the South, which occurred only during the decade of the thirties, was offset to some degree by the decline in the birthrate, the demand for school facilities was intensified as the proportion of Negro children attending school continued to climb.

The South entered the 1930's with Negro school attendance proportionately as great as that of the whites for the first time; the 2.4 million Negro pupils comprised about one-fourth of the total enrollment. Negroes were, however, attending shorter terms for the most part and they were still leaving school earlier, although the number of Negro high schools had risen from 67 in 1916 to 1,860 in 1928. Thus there was still a natural growth in the demand for schooling and in one way the depression provided greater opportunity for it. There was less cotton to be picked, or there was less reason for picking it, and the day had abruptly passed when every white family down to the lower reaches of the middle class could afford one or more Negro domestics. For many a Negro youth there was literally nothing to do except go to school—and Negro high school enrollment shot up to five times the 1920 peak. Lack of facilities probably prevented an even more dramatic increase. In parts of the rural South where the population was predominantly Negro well over half the high schools were reserved for whites. In 1933, more than 200 counties with Negro populations of 12.5 per cent or more still had no Negro high schools at all.

Lack of employment was having its effect on white attendance figures too; white youths, like their Negro contemporaries, were staying in school longer. Thus the South found itself in the impossible position of trying to educate one-third of the nation's children in a dual school system supported by only one-sixth of the nation's school revenue. Current operating expenditure per pupil stood at $45 during the decade—less than one-half the national figure. Building and maintenance funds were even more limited. In 1939-40, after the back of the depression was broken, the South was putting only $6 per pupil into capital expenditures, as against $14 for the rest of the nation.

Since the schools were dependent largely upon local tax sources, the rural schools fared far worse than those in the cities, where such wealth as the depression had spared was largely concentrated. The decade saw a substantial increase in state equalization funds intended to pull the rural schools up to minimum standards, and a great drive toward school consolidation in the hope of improving services at lower cost. Even so in the early and mid-thirties many rural school systems broke down completely. And as it had in the early days of public education, the South had to rely heavily on outside aid—this time in the form of grants from the depression-born alphabetical agencies of the New Deal. Of the $21 million the federal government spent directly to meet the rural school emergency between 1933 and 1935, 80 per cent went to the South. Rural schools also received a disproportionately large share of the $200 million provided for Southern school construction by the Public Works Administration. However, the cumulative deficiency was so great that even infusions of outside money on this scale could not check the general decline.

The rural schools in general were at the bottom of the heap, and the rural Negro schools—which still served two-thirds of the South's Negro children—occupied the very lowest stratum. With rare exceptions, these schools had never reached minimum standards in their best days, and now they were subject to financial malnutrition, overcrowding, and official neglect. The authorities who headed up the dual system continued to give them lowest priority—which in these desperate times often meant virtually no support at all. A measure of this is seen in the fact that Negro school projects accounted for only 8 per cent of the PWA school construction applications filed by state and local officials—who, of course, had to find matching money from withered local sources.

By the mid-point of the decade Negro pupils made up 30 per cent of the South's total school attendance, but the value of Negro school property in the dual system was only about 8 per cent of the total. More than half of all rural Negro schools were primitive one-room frame structures, wholly lacking in modern facilities. And many classes met in churches, lodge halls, or the abandoned tenant houses that marked the march of depression across the countryside.

In the non-South the economic decline took its toll of public education too—but there the Negro fared little worse than his white counterpart. Indeed, in one way he may even be said to have benefited. In most of the Northern cities segregation in the public schools had become more the product of residential pattern than of official policy. The Negroes who had flocked north and west in the twenties had concentrated in the older areas of the larger cities, and there they had taken over former white schools which, if they were inferior to those serving white students in the newer sections, were still better than any they had known. As migration from the South dropped to its lowest point since World War I, the pressure on these schools eased for the first time in 20 years.

The impact of the depression on the nation's public education structure increased in intensity from top to bottom—which meant that in many material ways the Negro schools suffered most. Yet, on the whole, Negro education continued to make steady progress through the period, and at the end there was more on the credit than on the debit side of the ledger. The facilities available to the race were grossly inade-

quate, and the standards were generally lower than those of
the white schools, but despite this Negro attendance continued to grow. The length of the Negro school term in
1939-40 was well above the 1929-30 figure. Negro teachers'
salaries were substantially higher, and although they were
still well below the white level the gap had been narrowed.
And Negroes were staying in school longer than ever before;
between 1920 and 1940 the proportion of total Negro attendance in the high school grades had risen from 2 to 10 per cent.

But by far the most important of the gains in Negro education in the thirties was the white leadership's increasing recognition of its responsibility for maintaining it. There was a
significant change in prevailing Southern attitudes between
the beginning and the end of the decade. After the shock of
the depression had worn off and the process of federal-
stimulated recovery had begun, Americans everywhere
tended to subject their democratic institutions to serious
re-examination. It was an era of liberalism in politics, and
the federal government was paying more attention to the
status of the Negro than it had since Reconstruction. It was
a time, too, when improving communications were breaking
down the South's traditional isolation; the automobile brought
the most remote farm within easy reach of the cities, newspaper and magazine circulation spread away from the rail
lines, and network radio's carefully neutral accents could be
heard in all parts of the land. Ideas which had heretofore
reached the South only through the filter of its own leadership now arrived intact and left their mark.

There were no revolutionary changes, to be sure. The
double standard around which the bi-racial school system
had been shaped survived the thirties, but it was being considered now in a new light. White leaders of standing began
to question openly the validity of a system which operated
on the theory that Negroes were entitled to only a limited

education, presumably tailored to a permanently truncated opportunity for economic advancement. If it were not yet to be followed in practice the "separate but equal" doctrine began to gain acceptance in its literal meaning as a policy. And there arose a school of "gradualism" whose adherents argued that, while the time for basic changes in racial relationships may not have arrived, all public policies in regard to the Negro should be shaped to the end that he would ultimately be equipped for and admitted to full citizenship.

Negro leadership had found an eloquent voice in DuBois and a skilled organizer in Walter White, and the National Association for the Advancement of Colored People was urging an increasingly militant stand against all forms of segregation. But within the South the Negro continued to play an essentially passive role in his own educational progress. It was, after all, hardly a propitious moment to question the legality of the obvious and admitted inequalities of the dual school system. Any Southern Negro leader who looked about him in the early thirties had to recognize that not even the most stringent court order could extract blood from the shriveled turnip upon which the whole school system depended for sustenance.

Except for a few scattered lawsuits of no particular consequence the legal weapon forged by the *Plessy* dictum remained sheathed during the thirties so far as the public schools of the South were concerned. On the level of higher education, however, two significant precedents were set in cases originating in the border states of Missouri and Maryland—litigation which would lead within a few years to the breaching of the wall of segregation in the graduate schools of the South. And on another front forces were gathering for the legal attack which in the forties would return the franchise to the Negro and have indirect but far-reaching effects upon the structure of bi-racial education.

CHAPTER FOUR

A New Look at the Fourteenth Amendment

IT WAS NOT UNTIL 1935, ALMOST FORTY YEARS AFTER THE Supreme Court handed down its historic ruling permitting separate but equal public educational facilities, that the *Plessy* doctrine was literally applied by Court order. The case arose in a border state, and the action was aimed at the top level of the public educational structure.

In that year Donald Murray, a Negro, applied for admission to the law school of the University of Maryland at Baltimore, and was duly refused in accordance with Maryland's segregation statutes. Murray went into state court with a complaint based on the fact that Maryland provided no law school for Negroes within its boundaries, but attempted to meet the *Plessy* doctrine by offering a limited number of scholarships for Negroes in institutions outside the state. The Maryland Court of Appeals upheld Murray's contention that the fifty scholarships available were not sufficient to insure that every qualified Negro applicant would receive one. Moreover, the Court accepted the argument that these scholarships, which covered only the cost of tuition, placed Negro students who must live away from home at an economic disadvantage.

The Court ordered Murray admitted to the Maryland law

school. It held the scholarship arrangement discriminatory, but it made the point that since no officials of Maryland were authorized to set up a separate law school, the Court did not have the power to order such an institution established. Therefore, the only remedy by which Murray could realize equal treatment was admission to the existing institution. The Maryland court scrupulously avoided re-defining the *Plessy* precedent, but it opened up important new avenues of relief when it specified non-segregation as a remedy when no other was readily available.

In its first significant application of *Plessy* in the field of higher education, the United States Supreme Court materially broadened the interpretation under which the state court had ordered Murray's admission to the University of Maryland. The *Gaines* case in 1938 was the real forerunner of the decisions of the forties which would open the doors of graduate schools in the South to Negroes. Lloyd Gaines sued for admission to the law school of the University of Missouri on the grounds that no separate law school for Negroes was provided in the state, and that the out-of-state scholarships available to him did not satisfy the requirement of equal treatment. The Supreme Court reversed the courts of Missouri in an opinion which announced a new point of law:

The basic consideration is not as to what sort of opportunities other states provide, or whether they are as good as those in Missouri, but as to what opportunities Missouri itself furnishes to white students and denies to Negroes solely upon the ground of color.... Manifestly, the obligation of the state to give the protection of equal laws can be performed only where its laws operate, that is, within its own jurisdiction.... Nor can we regard the fact that there is but limited demand in Missouri for the legal education of Negroes as excusing the discrimination in favor of whites.... Here petitioner's right was a personal one. It was as an individual that he was entitled to the equal protection of the laws, and the state was bound to furnish him within its borders facilities for legal education substantially equal to those which the state has afforded for persons of the white race. . . .

Thus the Court removed the legal basis for providing out-of-state scholarships for Negro applicants for specialized training, although in the absence of court challenge the device is still being employed in many states. The Court also laid new emphasis upon the personal rights of the applicant. Nevertheless, it still honored *Plessy* by not directly ordering Gaines admitted to the University, requiring only appropriate action to grant him equality of educational opportunity within the state. The case was sent back to the Missouri courts for execution of the order and when it finally came to rehearing in 1940 Gaines had dropped out of sight and the action ended there. However, after the hiatus of the war years, the *Gaines* precedent came to serve as the basis for further litigation which systematically widened the breach in the wall of segregation.

The *Sipuel* case, initiated against the University of Oklahoma in 1946, hinged upon the *Gaines* case, and brought forth another significant point of law. After Ada Lois Sipuel demonstrated that Oklahoma maintained no law school for Negroes, the United States Supreme Court held that the state must provide her with opportunity for a legal education—and added that it must do so as soon as it did for any other qualified applicant. The course of appeal had consumed two years, and the court order came to Oklahoma authorities by telegraph on January 12, 1948, exactly two weeks before the second term of law school was scheduled to open at Norman. The University regents announced that Langston University, the state Negro college, would establish a law school at Oklahoma City in time to receive Miss Sipuel. And so it did, with a faculty of three white lawyers assigned to teach her in rooms at the state capitol. She refused to accept this one-woman education, but the Supreme Court denied further relief on the technical ground that the question of segregation was not before it, and that the manner in which its previous mandate was carried out was a matter for the state courts to decide.

Miss Sipuel started the legal machinery all over again, and was finally admitted to the University of Oklahoma in 1949. But in the meantime another Negro applicant had carried a separate legal attack all the way to the point of admission at Norman. He was G. W. McLaurin, an elderly professor emeritus at Langston, who in 1948 took his demand for admission to the University graduate school of education to the federal district court in Oklahoma City. A special three-judge panel held that he was entitled to admission to the only graduate courses in his field offered by the state, and the University bowed to the order. In the wake of the *McLaurin* case the Oklahoma Legislature amended the state law to permit the admission of Negroes to the University for enrollment in those courses not offered by Langston. But at the same time, the legislature stipulated that segregation should be maintained on the campus, and McLaurin was required to sit apart from white students in the classroom, the library, and the dining hall. In 1949 McLaurin went back to federal court, alleging that these restrictions violated the equal protection provisions of the Fourteenth Amendment. The district court ruled against him, but on appeal the Supreme Court moved another significant step away from its old interpretation of *Plessy*. The restrictions placed upon McLaurin, it held, "impair and inhibit his ability to study, to engage in discussions and exchange views with other students, and, in general, to learn his profession." The Court concluded: "Appellant, having been admitted to a state-supported school, must receive the same treatment at the hands of the state as students of other races."

On the same day, June 5, 1950, the Supreme Court based an opinion in the case of *Sweatt* v. *Painter* on premises so broad as virtually to preclude separate education on the graduate and professional level.

Heman Sweatt's application for admission to the University of Texas law school was made in 1946 and resulted in a state court order holding that he was entitled to relief. The court, however, granted the state six months in which to set up a law school substantially equal to that of the University at Austin. The new institution was completed on schedule, but Sweatt refused to enroll and launched an appeal. He fought his case through the Texas courts without success until 1949, when the United States Supreme Court agreed to hear it. The *Sweatt* case differed importantly from all the others in that the plaintiff's legal staff, provided by the National Association for the Advancement of Colored People, for the first time made a frontal attack on the validity of segregation statutes *per se*. His attorneys not only attempted to show that the new Negro law school was materially inferior, but offered testimony by anthropologists, educators, and others to the effect that the Negro is as capable of learning as the white, that classification of students by race is arbitrary and unjust, and that segregation is harmful to personality development. In sum, they argued that no segregated Negro school could actually provide equal educational opportunity, and the Court obviously gave weight to their contention. In its opinion in the *Sweatt* case the Court not only found the Negro law school inferior in terms of number of faculty, variety of courses, scope of library and other usual measurements, but it went on to say, in an opinion written by the late Chief Justice Fred Vinson:

What is more important, the University of Texas Law School possesses to a far greater degree those qualities which are incapable of objective measurement but which make for greatness in a law school. Such qualities, to name but a few, include reputation of the faculty, experience of the administration, position and influence of the alumni, standing in the community, traditions and prestige.

Few if any existing state Negro colleges in the South could meet the tests here posed by the Court, and obviously no brand new institution, jumped up under the threat of court order, could demonstrate the position and influence of its alumni, or point with pride to its traditions and prestige.

In the *Sipuel, McLaurin* and *Sweatt* cases, though failing to overturn the *Plessy* doctrine, the Court had ruled out segregation in specific instances and had largely invalidated it in the field of graduate and professional training.

In June, 1947, the Board of Trustees of the University of Arkansas, plainly aware of the course of litigation in the bordering states although there was no threat of a suit in Arkansas, voluntarily ruled that henceforth qualified Negro applicants would be admitted to those courses not offered by the state-supported Negro college at Pine Bluff. The practical effect of the new policy was to limit Negro enrollment to the graduate and professional schools. On February 1, 1948, Silas Hunt was enrolled in the School of Law at Fayetteville. He was the first Negro to enter a public university in any of the former Confederate states since Reconstruction.

Meanwhile, the Southern states had pooled resources to set up a regional program for higher education. Through an inter-state compact, they agreed to cooperate in the establishment of strong centers of graduate and professional training which would draw students of both races from all the participating states. From its inception the plan was denounced by many Negro leaders as a device for preserving segregation at the university level. Officials of the Board of Control for Southern Regional Education—now called the Southern Regional Education Board—denied the charge and provided affirmative evidence to refute it when the board intervened in a test of segregation at the University of Maryland in 1949. The state had defended its exclusion of a Negro from the university's school of nursing by pointing out that she was entitled to out-of-state training at Meharry Medical School under the regional education compact. The SREB, speaking as a "friend of the court," declared: "It is not the Board's purpose that the regional program shall serve any state as legal defense for avoiding responsibilities under the existing state and federal laws and court decisions." The lower court ruled against the Negro applicant, but the decision was reversed by the Maryland Court of Appeals, which ordered her admitted to the state university.

While spokesmen for the NAACP have continued to criticize the regional education program, it is clear that it has not served as a legal device to preserve segregation. Since 1949, with a spattering of litigation to spur the process, twenty previously segregated public institutions have admitted Negroes. At the beginning of the 1953 term only five state universities still had not opened their doors to Negroes—those in Mississippi, Alabama, Georgia, Florida, and South Carolina. For the most part the new Negro students have been enrolled in graduate and professional courses; the only significant exception is at the University of Louisville, which in 1951 absorbed a city-supported Negro college and in effect integrated the two undergraduate student bodies. Since few if any of these institutions maintain student records by race, it is impossible to fix the exact number of Negroes who have been admitted to formerly-segregated universities during these four years, but the best available estimate is that between 1,000 and 2,000 have been enrolled during regular sessions. If summer school attendance is taken into account, the total figure is probably three to four times as large. Moreover, thirteen private or church-related institutions, twelve Protestant theological seminaries, and twenty-one Catholic institutions in Southern and border states have followed the pattern established in the public universities, even though they are presumably beyond the reach of court action.

This is, of course, only a small percentage of the total of about 700,000 students enrolled annually in Southern institutions of higher education between 1948 and 1952. Even so the presence of this comparative handful of Negroes in these institutions represents a significant change in the long-standing educational pattern in the United States.

Was the process by which they crossed the color bar evolutionary or, as many white Southerners somewhat loosely charged, "revolutionary"? Certainly the initial assault upon the upper ramparts of the segregated educational structure was carefully planned and executed. The several plaintiffs in the early cases were as thoughtfully selected as the legal grounds they chose to test, with NAACP attorneys appearing in every instance. Moreover, the NAACP made it quite plain that the education cases were part of a two-pronged attack in its continuing campaign against segregation—the other being the successful drive against restrictions on the ballot which by 1948 had destroyed the "white primary" and removed the last important legal barriers to the franchise. Even so, it was a natural process that made the higher education cases possible, and very probably inevitable. By the end of the thirties the Negro wing of the dual educational structure was finally built up to the point where a sizable and steadily increasing number of Negroes were moving all the way through the educational pipe line from the first grade through the fourth year of undergraduate training. Not until 1939 did any of the Southern states attempt to provide graduate and professional training in the Negro wing of the dual system to bolster that available in a few private Negro institutions. The result was that the South was faced with a legitimate and growing demand for upper-level education it could not meet, even under the most liberal construction of the *Plessy* doctrine, except at exorbitant cost. Something had to give, and it turned out to be the wall of segregation.

CHAPTER FIVE

Racial Integration at the University Level

IN JUNE, 1938, THE FIRST NEGRO TO CROSS THE COLOR LINE IN higher education under court order was graduated twelfth in a class of thirty-seven at the University of Maryland School of Law. Donald Murray subsequently wrote:

My experience, briefly, was that I attended the University of Maryland Law School for three years, during which time I took all of the classes with the rest of the students . . . and at no time whatever did I meet any attempted segregation or unfavorable treatment on the part of any student in the school, or any professor or assistant professor.

Donald Murray's experience is typical of that of most of the Negro students who followed him into the previously segregated universities of the South and the border states. This does not mean that there has not been a considerable variation in the treatment accorded Negro students in the course of the South's first significant experience with integrated education. But in most cases there was a marked contrast in official attitudes before and after the fact of Negro admission.

All the Southern universities firmly excluded Negro students until the Supreme Court had systematically undercut the legal basis of their admission policies. It is impossible to determine how often this represented the attitude of university administrators, and how often it only reflected passive acceptance of existing statutes and prevailing public opinion. In any event, it must be noted that no university administration in the South, public or private, actively sought to abandon segregation until it was faced with what its board of trustees could agree was the inevitable.

Some universities—or at least the state officials who appear in court on their behalf—are still resisting. In November of 1953 Louisiana State University cancelled the previous registration of the first Negro undergraduate in its history after a federal appeals court reversed the lower court injunction which had gained him admission. The university announced that it was taking this action in accordance with its official policy of admitting Negroes only in compliance with court decisions.

Yet LSU has had Negroes on its campus ever since 1950—eight of them in its graduate schools in the first semester of 1952-53 and twelve in the second. The 1953 summer session had a Negro enrollment of 104. All these Negro students did not, of course, individually sue for admission, but the University apparently accepted the fact that they could have under the precedents of the *Gaines, McLaurin,* and *Sweatt* cases—while the university still feels that it can hold the line in the case of an undergraduate to whom comparable courses are available at the state-supported Negro college.

Those Negroes who do get past the legal barrier at LSU are officially accorded treatment equal with that enjoyed by white students. They live in regular student dormitories, with no amendment to the usual rules except that under the "principle of compatibility" administrators so far have not assigned a Negro and a white student to room together. Negroes sit where they please in dining halls, the cafeteria and coffee shop, and use the field house and other facilities on the same basis as white students. No Negro student has yet entered the swimming pool or attended a dance—although the administration has indicated that it would protect his right to do so.

With only a few exceptions, the pattern at LSU is typical of all the Southern universities—official resistance to Negro admission until, voluntarily or as the result of court action, the admission policy is changed; even-handed application of administrative policies once Negroes are admitted. This does not mean that the limited integration at these Southern institutions has been accomplished without incident. Field studies on seventeen of the twenty-two integrated campuses in the summer of 1953 turned up several instances of near-friction, but none had reached the serious stage. Professor Guy B. Johnson of the University of North Carolina, who directed these studies, concluded that on the whole the process of transition and adjustment to new racial patterns on the college campuses could be adjudged a peaceful one. In a postscript to his report he wrote:

> In almost every instance when a state institution was faced with the fact that it might actually have to admit Negroes, there were serious predictions of violence and bloodshed *if* this thing came to pass. To the best of our knowledge, the first drop of blood is yet to be shed.

The attitude of faculties toward the new Negro students has been generally sympathetic. In 1946, when the University of Kentucky was faced with the prospect of admitting Negroes, Theodore Wirth, a graduate student, made a confidential survey of faculty attitudes as preparation for his master's thesis. He found that 60 per cent of the faculty favored removing all legal restrictions to non-segregated education, with only 22 per cent opposed. Only 11 per cent of the faculty members said they would find the presence of Negroes in their classrooms offensive. On the question of whether there was a racial difference in intellectual ability, 66 per cent said no, 7 per cent said yes, and 26 per cent did not know.

Actual experience with Negroes in their classrooms appears to have created no unpleasantness for faculty members at Kentucky or elsewhere, but it has raised special problems. There is universal agreement that the Negro students are handicapped by their generally inferior educational background. Very few faculty members intimate that this reflects any sort of racial trait; rather there is a frank facing of the fact that few Southern Negroes have the prior scholastic training which would enable them to compete on equal terms with white students—and some of those who do have such training still go outside the South for their graduate or professional studies. A few have performed well, but the majority have fallen below the average of academic achievement.

Against the special background of the early days of Negro admission to Southern universities this has posed a dilemma for many teachers. If a faculty member grades the Negro student by exactly the same standard he applies to the whites, he is up against the cold fact that he will be flunking a high proportion of the Negroes in his classes. Thus he will run the risk of being accused of discrimination. At the University of North Carolina several Negro law students were listed as having unsatisfactory grades in the 1951-52 session, and a NAACP spokesman at nearby Durham charged publicly that there had been discrimination in grading. The Law School faculty denied the charge, pointing out that the examination papers in question were identified only by number, and later one of the students concerned was reported in the press to have told an NAACP gathering that he felt the grade discrepancy was due solely to the poor academic background of the Negro students. Impartial investigation by persons strongly opposed to segregation of Negroes in law schools bears this out. This incident is the only one of its kind reported, but it is indicative of the special considerations that enter into the white teacher-Negro student relationship. The result is an apparent tendency toward easier or more "sympathetic" grading of Negro students as compensation for their academic handicaps. There is less indication of this in medical and law schools than in other departments.

On the whole the white students have been either indifferent or sympathetic to their newly arrived Negro colleagues. There has been very little overt rudeness or antagonism expressed toward them. On some of the campuses a small minority is quite bitter about having the Negroes around, and on the other extreme there is usually a small minority which takes an active, friendly interest in their welfare.

The prevailing Southern mores make it difficult for wholly normal, give-and-take relationships to grow up between white and Negro students. On one hand white students are afraid that they might unintentionally offend the Negroes, and on the other they are aware of the social risk if they are overly friendly. The least strained relationships have grown up at professional schools with more or less isolated campuses. There the smaller and more mature student bodies tend to carry over their informal working relationships outside the classrooms. Intimate social contact, however, is rare, because of abstract reasons of custom and the concrete fact that segregation still is rigidly observed in those off-campus resorts where students normally gather.

White students, as individuals and in groups, have sometimes taken the lead on behalf of equal privileges for Negroes both on and off campus. This tendency has been particularly marked at Oklahoma A & M, the University of Missouri, and the University of Kansas City. At the University of Arkansas a special mark of approbation was given a Negro law student when he was elected president of his predominantly white dormitory. In the main, however, the white students have maintained a detachment bordering on disinterest. It is noteworthy that there is virtually no evidence that Communist or Communist-front groups have tried to exploit the more sensitive aspects of the situation on any campus.

In their turn the Negro students have generally worked hard to avoid imposing undue strain on a relationship they recognize to be delicate. The first Negroes to enter each institution usually had a strong sense of their importance as "pioneers"—a sense reinforced by the fact that most Negro community leaders were aware of the crucial nature of those early admissions and generally tried to see to it that studious, restrained persons blazed the trail. Southern Negro leaders are still actively discouraging inferior students and "trouble makers" from seeking admission to the interracial campuses, and encouraging those they believe will be "a credit to the race." Only three notable failures among the "pioneers" were noted in the seventeen field studies in the Johnson report: The first Negro law student flunked out of the University of Texas; the man whose lawsuit opened the University of Virginia to Negroes dropped out without completing his studies; and the first entrant at Louisiana State withdrew after it was discovered that he had been dishonorably discharged from the army.

The official discriminations that marked the treatment of Negroes on some campuses in the early days have now disappeared except for occasional special arrangements in dormitories. A scale of the degree of equality of participation in campus life by Negro students would range from the high-

DAVID N. MIELKE

est point in academic work to the lowest in their relations with the outside community.

University administrators, being more exposed to public pressures, tend to be more cautious and conservative in politically sensitive matters than either faculty or students—and so they are in the case of their new Negro students. Official attitudes vary from a firm stand in favor of full integration of Negro students to a somewhat grudging concession of minimum accommodations and privileges. In practically all the schools surveyed administrators indicated their interest in holding down the number of Negro enrollees, or at least in making sure that any increase in Negro attendance is gradual. This may be one of the reasons no state institution has yet admitted any out-of-state Negro student—which the court decisions apparently do not compel them to do. This is not to suggest that there has been any widespread manipulation of entrance standards or other resort to "administrative runaround." Actually, the demand for admission has been so small that there has been no real problem, and the administrators' concern is primarily a reflection of their sensitivity to public opinion. For the same reason they have usually sought to limit or at least control publicity about their Negro students. The general attitude of the administrators might be expressed as the hope that everybody on the outside will forget that Negroes are on the campus—which, as a matter of fact, usually has been the practical result once the first flurry attendant upon their initial admission has subsided.

The South's experience with integrated higher education is broad enough and has continued long enough to have considerable significance. It must be recognized, however, that the experience is limited in important ways. For the most part, Negro admissions have been confined to the graduate and professional schools. This in itself is a selective process, and on top of it the Negro community has often exerted a positive influence to screen out undesirables. The number of Negroes has not yet grown proportionately large on any campus, which tends to reduce the possibility of racial tension. On the other side, the first Southern whites to experience integration in education on their home grounds have done so at the upper levels and are of a generation which has personally experienced the re-orientation of World War II.

For these reasons, and perhaps others, there has been remarkably little public protest against the new policies in the institutions of higher learning. Nowhere has the admission of Negroes produced anything like a boycott, nor has it been made a prime political issue. The Southern public has not cheered integration in the graduate schools, but neither has it condemned it out of hand. White Southerners in the states which have adopted such policies seem to look upon the admission of Negroes to their universities as a problem, but a manageable one, and nobody in the region seriously expects to see the tide turned back.

CHAPTER SIX

The Deep-Running Currents of Change

IN THE CONTEXT OF THE FORTIES THE COURT-ORDERED ADMISSION of the first Negroes to hitherto segregated universities was only a minor manifestation of the huge forces that were buffeting the whole of American public education. There was the war, which first stripped the college campuses of students and then overburdened them with military trainees and a flood of returning GIs. There was the shortage of essential materials which halted school building before the ravages of the depression could be repaired, and the post-war boom which brought the greatest income the schools had ever known, and the inflation which promptly devalued it. There was the erratic birthrate during the years of fighting, and the record crop of post-war babies. There was the final breakdown of natural isolation as young men and women were called forth from the farms and villages and dispatched over most of the world. There was the sudden emergence of the United States as the ranking power in an uneasy world. Above all, there were the great internal migrations, which affected the United States as though a giant egg beater had been inserted into the center of its population.

This great shaking up had profound meaning for the Negro. If it did not dislodge him from the bottom of the economic and social scale, it at least opened up great gaps above him. He went into a wholly segregated military service at the beginning of the decade, but ten years later Jim Crow had been officially drummed out of the armed forces and the Negro was fighting shoulder to shoulder with white troops on the bloody ridges of Korea. He regained the franchise in those states which had denied him access to the polls for half a century, and by 1950 he could count more than a million eligible Negro voters in the South. In 1947 he saw a presidential Committee on Civil Rights flatly recommend

. . . the elimination of segregation, based on race, color, creed, or national origin, from American life. The separate but equal doctrine has failed in three important respects. First, it is inconsistent with the fundamental equalitarianism of the American way of life in that it marks groups with the brand of inferior status. Secondly, where it has been followed, the results have been separate and unequal facilities for minority peoples. Finally, it has kept people apart despite incontrovertible evidence that an environment favorable to civil rights is fostered whenever groups are permitted to live and work together. There is no adequate defense of segregation.

The Truman administration did not succeed in implementing this recommendation with specific legislation, but neither did it abandon it—even though in 1948 it faced a major political rebellion and saw a protesting third party arise briefly in the South. Nor has the Republican party dissented from the principles set forth in the 1947 Civil Rights report; the new regime in Washington has not pressed for implementing legislation since it came to power, but by executive order it has been systematically rooting out the vestiges of segregation in all federal establishments. In furtherance of policies laid down in tentative fashion under the Truman administration, by the beginning of the 1953 school term segregation had been ended in all schools operated by the Defense Department for the children of military personnel. This meant integration in elementary and/or high schools at Army, Navy, or Marine establishments in Virginia, North Carolina, South Carolina, Georgia, and Kentucky. The military was still permitting segregation in post schools operated on contract by local school officials in Alabama, Arkansas, Florida, Maryland, Oklahoma, South Carolina, Texas, and Virginia. However, in early 1954 the Defense Department announced that these schools would be de-segregated by September 1, 1955—under federal operation if necessary.

The dual school system in the South was not immune to these deep-running currents of change. While the primary legal attack of the forties was directed toward admission of Negroes to institutions of higher education, the issue of inequality in the primary and secondary schools was also brought before the federal courts a dozen times. The courts consistently held with the *Plessy* precedent, but they began interpreting "separate but equal" with increasing stringency. In *Corbin* v. *County School Board of Pulaski County, Virginia* the court declared that the question of inequality "cannot be decided by averaging the facilities provided for the two classes of pupils throughout the county and comparing one with the other, since the rights created by the Fourteenth Amendment are . . . observed only when the same or equivalent treatment is accorded to persons of different races similarly situated."

In these post-war cases the courts not only set up increasingly rigid standards by which they compared the separate schools, but they cast themselves in a supervisory role in enforcing their orders. In the *Smith* case arising in King George County, Virginia, the court found inequalities of physical facilities and curricula between the white and Negro high schools, and ordered immediate equalization. The court held that neither the poor financial condition of the school district nor the disproportionate amount of school taxes paid by the whites had any bearing on the case. Subsequently, when improvements to the Negro school proved inadequate, the Negro plaintiffs petitioned for a contempt citation. Before the court acted, however, school authorities attempted to "equalize down" by dropping certain courses at the white high school—a step which evoked protests from both white and Negro parents. A bond issue, which had previously been rejected by the voters, was then approved and an acceptable equalization program was worked out in the sort of court-supervised conference that came to be widely employed.

These court tests made it clear that if segregation was to be maintained in the public schools equality in the dual system would have to be a fact, not a token policy. In the late forties many of the states appropriated additional funds for equalization programs and stipulated that there must be no discrimination in their expenditure by the school districts. In most of the cities teachers' pay scales were equalized, and everywhere the gap was narrowed. It is noteworthy that the greatest effort at the state level has been expended in states where the Negro population is heaviest, and where political leaders have manifested the greatest concern over the threat to segregation in education. South Carolina and Georgia have enacted special new taxes and earmarked all or part of their proceeds for school improvement programs designed to wipe out inequalities in the dual system. A similar effort has been made in Mississippi, although there Governor Hugh White encountered greater resistance from his legislature. In South Carolina, where Governor James F. Byrnes has launched what properly has been called "an educational revolution," some $84 million of a projected $176 million has been allocated for school construction since 1951, and 69 per cent of it has gone to Negro schools. Appropriations for operating expenses also have been almost doubled. In his inaugural address on January 16, 1951, the governor said: "It is our duty to provide for the races substantial equality in school facilities. We should do it because it is right. For me that is sufficient reason."

Governor Byrnes very probably bespoke the prevailing attitude of a majority of Southern whites—but the goal of separate equality has not always been pursued so vigorously as in South Carolina. Efforts to obtain equalization funds from state legislatures, or to pass special bond issues in local school districts, have run into keen competition with other demands for expanded services. The post-war boom has brought the South the greatest prosperity it has ever known, but it has also created new needs, particularly in those areas where industrialization is proceeding rapidly. In the forties the region was also called upon to build highways, hospitals, and water and sewer systems at an unprecedented rate.

Throughout the decade the South was still building a total educational structure that had never caught up with the growing demand for schooling, and despite the great economic gains of the period the region was hampered by a per capita income that remained at the bottom of the national scale. Moreover, the human base of the structure was shifting far more rapidly than most Southerners realized and creating special new problems in the process.

All Americans were affected to some degree by the push and pull of the war years, but the migration of Negro population was without parallel. In the decade after 1940 the re-distribution of Negro population was greater than in all the preceding years combined.

Three main streams of Negro migration were evident, and all had a direct and important bearing on educational opportunities for the minority race:

1. The mass exodus of Negroes from the South to the big cities of the non-South.

2. The movement of Negroes from Southern rural farm areas, where they had been traditionally concentrated, to the urban areas of the South.

3. The increasing density of Negroes in the older, central sections of the cities to which they moved.

At the end of the decade it was clear that the Negro's future would be increasingly identified with the cities, a sociological change of great significance. Moreover, the spread of Negro population over the whole country—with a corresponding proportionate decrease in concentration in the South—gave his special problems for the first time a genuinely national rather than a regional character. The Negro migration in the forties was only a continuation of trends that had been in existence for more than 30 years, but it now reached a point where it could only be regarded as one of the last steps in the uprooting of an old culture and the beginning of a new era in race relations.

More than one million Negroes left the South between 1940 and 1950. The region's gain in Negro population was less than 150,000, the smallest since the World War I decade, while outside the South the Negro population rose by two million. Most of the non-Southern increases were recorded in seven states—Illinois, Ohio, and Michigan in the midwest; New York, New Jersey, and Pennsylvania in the northeast; California on the west coast; and the District of Columbia. In 1900 only one American Negro in eight lived outside the South, but by 1950 the proportion had risen to three in eight and the ratio was still increasing. (See Chart 2.)

In the South this trend was reversed, and the Negro became numerically less important. Between the turn of the century and 1950, the increase of white population in the South stood at 18 million, ten times the Negro increase. But between 1940 and 1950, the white increase of 4.5 million was

2 SHIFTS IN THE NEGRO POPULATION OF THE U. S. 1940 TO 1950

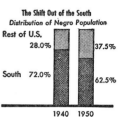

The Shift Out of the South
Distribution of Negro Population

Rest of U.S.   28.0%   37.5%

South   72.0%   62.5%

1940   1950

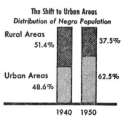

The Shift to Urban Areas
Distribution of Negro Population

Rural Areas   51.4%   37.5%

Urban Areas   48.6%   62.5%

1940   1950

SOME EXAMPLES OF THE SHIFT OUT OF THE SOUTH

Source: U. S. Census of 1950.

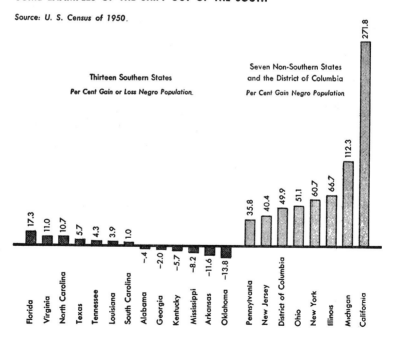

Thirteen Southern States
Per Cent Gain or Loss Negro Population.

Seven Non-Southern States and the District of Columbia
Per Cent Gain Negro Population

Florida 17.3
Virginia 11.0
North Carolina 10.7
Texas 5.7
Tennessee 4.3
Louisiana 3.9
South Carolina 1.0
Alabama –.4
Georgia –2.0
Kentucky –5.7
Mississippi –8.2
Arkansas –11.6
Oklahoma –13.8

Pennsylvania 35.8
New Jersey 40.4
District of Columbia 49.9
Ohio 51.1
New York 60.7
Illinois 66.7
Michigan 112.3
California 271.8

3 RECENT CHANGES IN THE SOUTH'S POPULATION

Per Cent Increase or Decrease, 1940-1950

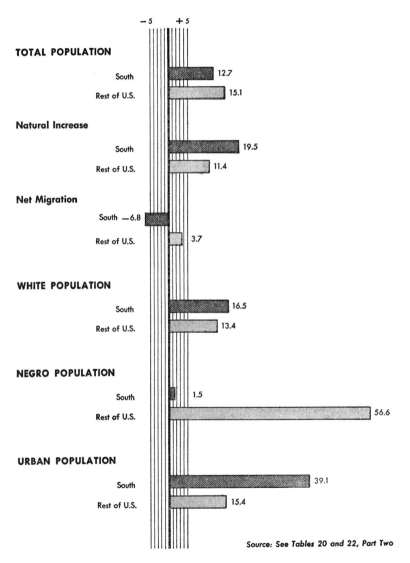

TOTAL POPULATION
South — 12.7
Rest of U.S. — 15.1

Natural Increase
South — 19.5
Rest of U.S. — 11.4

Net Migration
South — —6.8
Rest of U.S. — 3.7

WHITE POPULATION
South — 16.5
Rest of U.S. — 13.4

NEGRO POPULATION
South — 1.5
Rest of U.S. — 56.6

URBAN POPULATION
South — 39.1
Rest of U.S. — 15.4

Source: See Tables 20 and 22, Part Two

33 times as great as the Negro gain. (See Chart 3 and Tables 16-22.)

Overall, then, the South was growing whiter during the forties, and this trend was reflected in internal population shifts which were changing the face of the region. The great general exodus from the farms brought a decline in Negro farm population of 1.3 million. This was a process that had begun when the new era of agricultural mechanization first reduced the demand for farm labor, but it was sharply accelerated by the expanded industrial opportunity for Negroes during the war years and after. By the mid-forties the movement had so stripped the rural areas of their traditional labor supply that the cotton farmers of the Mississippi valley were importing migrant labor from Mexico to harvest their crops.

Many rural Negroes left the South entirely, never to return, but others moved only to the Southern cities. Even so the cities of the region without exception were growing whiter too, for the parallel trend of white rural migration sent far fewer whites permanently out of the South. The rural South lost proportionately fewer whites than Negroes, and the cities gained proportionately more.

Inside and outside the South the migrating Negroes headed for the larger metropolitan areas, and there the patterns of residential segregation channeled them into the central downtown districts. They came to rest in the decaying hearts of the great cities, overcrowding the older Negro neighborhoods and gradually pressing outward as the white population continued its mass movement to the suburbs. (See Chart 4.)

The great shift of Negro population had profound effects on public school education. The heavy pressure of Negro population was decreased in the rural South, where school facilities were least adequate. At the same time the towns and cities were faced with new demands for additional classroom space for Negro children. And beyond the population changes themselves, there was the continued rise in Negro attendance. Significant improvements in Negro family income and significant declines in the Negro infant mortality rate meant that a proportionately larger number of Negro children were going to school, and were staying in school longer.

During the 1940-1950 decade, average daily attendance in Southern schools increased 218,000. There was virtually no net gain in the rest of the nation, the rising school population on the west coast being offset by declines elsewhere, so the South's increasing school burden was nearly equal to the net increase for the United States as a whole. This took place in the face of an overall population gain in the South

---

The Changing Pattern in Southern Cities

The maps of Atlanta on pages 58 and 59 illustrate recent changes in the population and school distribution pattern of Southern cities.

Atlanta is a city of some 500,000 persons, approximately 32 per cent of whom are Negroes. It forms the core of a much larger metropolitan area. Eighty-nine per cent of Atlanta's Negro population is concentrated in the old central area of the city. The map on page 58 shows this concentration. The outline areas represent the Negro neighborhoods as they looked in 1930. The heavy black areas show Negro residental expansion since 1930.

In 1953 Atlanta had 106 public elementary and secondary schools, 32 of them for Negroes. The distribution of these schools, which corresponds to the distribution of white and Negro population, is shown on the map on page 59. In the heart of the city the map shows a heavy concentration of Negro schools, a cluster of Negro schools that were previously white, and a scatter of white schools in neighborhoods where Negro population is increasing. In the suburbs, where the white population has increased substantially in recent years, white schools predominate and there is a scatter of Negro schools in neighborhoods where white population is increasing.

Sources: Atlanta city directories for 1930 and for 1951-52; maps and records of the Metropolitan Planning Commission; records of the Atlanta Board of Education.

4   AN EXAMPLE OF THE CHANGING

1953 NEGRO RESIDENTIAL AREAS
ATLANTA, GEORGIA

☐   As of 1930
▰   Expansion since 1930
-----   Railroads
——   City Limits, 1952

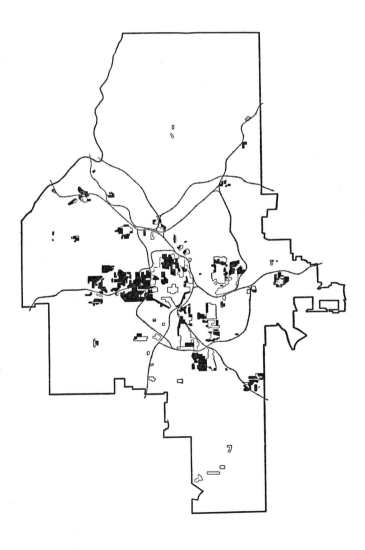

PATTERN IN SOUTHERN CITIES

1953 PUBLIC ELEMENTARY AND SECONDARY SCHOOLS
ATLANTA, GEORGIA

o   White school
●   Negro school
◉   Negro school, previously white
△   White school where Negro population is increasing
▲   Negro school where white population is increasing
↔   Railroads
—   City Limits, 1952

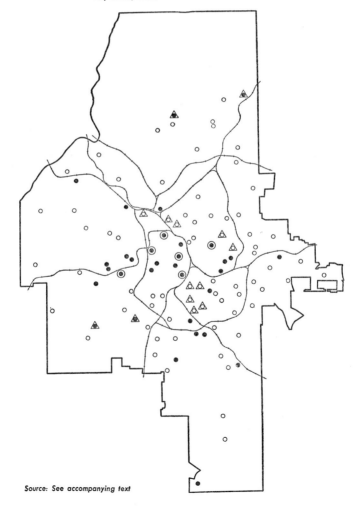

Source: See accompanying text

that was less rapid than that of other regions. Although total white population in the region rose 16.5 per cent between 1940 and 1950, white school attendance went up about 3 per cent. On the other hand, Negro school attendance also rose 3 per cent in the face of only 1.5 per cent increase in total Negro population. (See Chart 5.)

Thus the South was grappling with an increasing total school load even before the great post-war baby crop reached school age and created what educators came to call the "Battle of the Bulge."

Clearly visible in today's pattern of Negro school attendance in the South are two long-range population trends working in opposite directions. One is the continued increase in Negro urban population, with increased demands for more and better classrooms in the central sections of the cities—where the schools are generally old and might otherwise be passing out of existence to be replaced by new structures in the burgeoning suburbs. Here the problems of equalization are entangled with the intricate patterns of residential segregation. The other major trend is the marked drop of Negro population in the rural areas, which will inevitably bring about a large reduction of school attendance—and with it the economic problem of maintaining separate Negro schools for a steadily declining enrollment. So far the rural decline has been largely offset by the higher post-depression birthrate, the decreases in infant mortality and the increased attendance ratio. But when these influences have worn off rural Negro attendance is bound to begin a general decline—as it already has in a good many places.

Since 1940 the South has made its greatest efforts on behalf of public education, and it has given Negro children the largest share of the total outlay they have ever known. In 1951-52 the thirteen Southern states spent more than $1.2

5 WHITE AND NEGRO CHILDREN IN SOUTHERN SCHOOLS, 1952

There are wide variations state by state . . . . .

IN THE TOTAL NUMBER OF CHILDREN ATTENDING SCHOOL

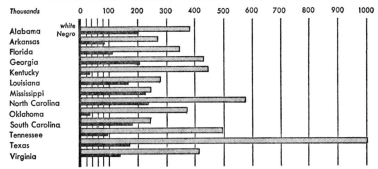

IN THE PROPORTION OF NEGRO TO WHITE CHILDREN

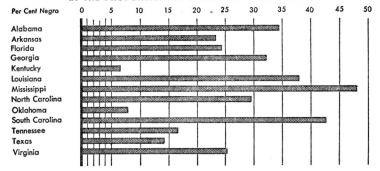

IN THE CHANGES IN SCHOOL ATTENDANCE FROM 1940 TO 1952

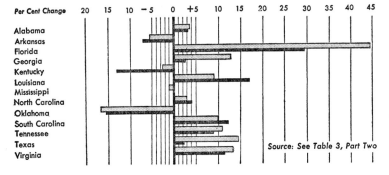

Source: See Table 3, Part Two

6   THE WHITE-NEGRO GAP IN SOUTHERN EDUCATION IS LARGE . . .

By most of these measures

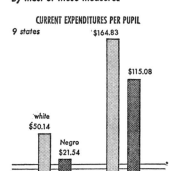

CURRENT EXPENDITURES PER PUPIL

9 states $164.83

$115.08

white $50.14

Negro $21.54

1940   1952

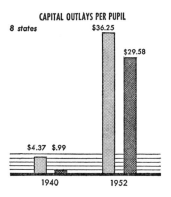

CAPITAL OUTLAYS PER PUPIL

8 states $36.25

$29.58

$4.37 $.99

1940   1952

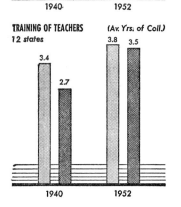

TRAINING OF TEACHERS   (Av. Yrs. of Coll.)

12 states   3.8   3.5

3.4

2.7

1940   1952

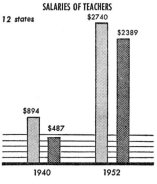

SALARIES OF TEACHERS

12 states $2740

$2389

$894

$487

1940   1952

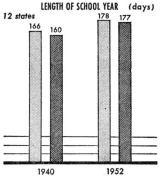

LENGTH OF SCHOOL YEAR   (days)

12 states   178   177

166   160

1940   1952

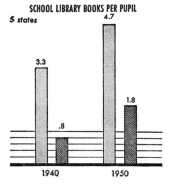

SCHOOL LIBRARY BOOKS PER PUPIL

5 states   4.7

3.3

.8

1.8

1940   1950

. . . . . BUT IT IS CLOSING

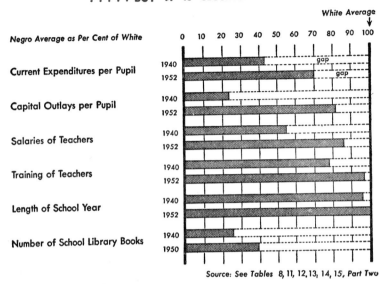

Source: See Tables 8, 11, 12, 13, 14, 15, Part Two

billion for school operations—nearly four times the expenditures for 1939-40. Of this amount, some $220 million went for Negro schools. Adjusting these figures to offset the effects of inflation, the operational expenditure for both races in 1951-52 was nearly twice as great as in the pre-war years. (See Tables 6-8.)

Over and above operating expenditures, the same states spent a total of nearly $315 million for school construction and maintenance in 1951-52—about eight times the amount spent in 1939-40. Between 1940 and 1952, the total value of school buildings rose from $1.2 billion to more than $3 billion; with adjustment for inflation this represents a net gain of nearly $1 billion. An estimated $65 to $70 million of the region's capital expenditures in 1951-52 went into Negro schools and equipment—and for the first time this amount approximated the 25 per cent proportion of Negro attendance.

Despite these accelerated efforts, however, the differential between white and Negro education in the region has remained large. For example, the Negro share of operating expenditures of 1951-52—some $220 million—was less than two-thirds of parity when measured against white and Negro attendance. The gap between current expenditures for whites and Negroes had been materially narrowed—but it was still wide: $115 per pupil in the Negro wing of the dual system, against $165 per pupil in the white wing. (See Chart 6.)

Specific measurements of the disparities between the two wings of the school system show varying results. In the overall pupil-teacher ratio the gap is almost closed—23.6 for white schools and 25.6 for Negro. So it is with the length of school terms. In 1939-40 nearly every state had a significant differential, but by 1951-52 no state showed a difference of as much as ten days.

In the matter of teachers' pay the gap had been cut more than half but it still stood at 15 per cent—$2,740 for whites against $2,389 for Negroes. Near equality had been attained in average figures for teacher training; measured in years of college experience the overall figures stood at 3.8 for whites and 3.5 for Negroes.

The Negro wing had fared worst in the matter of supplemental services. Although there had been a considerable increase in the total number of school libraries, the number of books available per Negro pupil was less than half the number per white pupil. The percentage of whites eating in federally-aided school lunchrooms was almost twice as great as Negroes, and the expenditure per pupil in average daily attendance showed that some $8 more per year was spent to feed the whites.

These overall figures, of course, smooth out great discrepancies in the performance of individual states. In the matter of total expenditure per pupil in average daily attendance, for example, the range was from a white-Negro ratio of 2½:1 to 11:10. There were also wide variations in teachers' salaries; in four of the states—Virginia, North Carolina, Oklahoma, and Tennessee—average salaries were higher for Negro teachers than for white. (See Tables 13 and 14.)

Thus the situation stood in the South when the Negro leadership laid its sights squarely on the *Plessy* doctrine and took five public school cases to the Supreme Court—the first the Court had consented to hear since *Gong Lum* v. *Rice* in 1927.

CHAPTER SEVEN

The Non-South: New Faces and New Problems

UNTIL WORLD WAR I THE HISTORY OF THE NEGRO OUTSIDE THE
South was largely the story of individuals and it had great
variety. Some of the first to arrive in the North came via the
Underground Railway in the days of abolitionist fervor and
were greeted as heroes. Others drifted in to arouse nothing
more than mild curiosity, which soon gave way to public
indifference. But as Negroes increased in numbers in the non-
Southern cities, gradually at first and then in a rising tide of
immigration, they encountered a familiar social phenomenon:
the larger the concentration of a minority group, the greater
the degree of discrimination.

In the beginning, the Negro's experience was not unlike
that of the other racial and religious minorities that fed the
growing population of the nation's great cities. As new ar-
rivals, the Jews, the Italians, the Poles, the Germans and the
Irish were herded into ghettoes and given access only to
menial jobs. But time eroded the language patterns and old
world customs which were the manifestations of their new-
ness, and with the passage of generations they spread outward from the older neighborhoods and rose upward in the
social order. The Negro, with his darker pigmentation, has

remained a "visible minority" and for him the initial patterns of segregation have endured.

Educational segregation in the non-South has been more the product of residential patterns than of law—although there is abundant evidence that many school administrators have adopted segregation as a conscious policy without formal sanction, and indeed in defiance of the statutes. Such practices as gerrymandering school districts, encouraging "voluntary" choice of separate schools by Negro pupils, carefully regulating transfer permits, and other comparable administrative arrangements have been common.

In recent years, however, there has been a strong countertrend. In some of the border states, laws prescribing or permitting some degree of educational segregation have been repealed or liberalized. In other states where the law has never condoned segregation, legal and administrative action has been directed toward elimination of the separate pattern. The forces that have led the South to a new recognition of the deficiencies of its dual school system have also been at work in the non-South, and there too they have had profound results.

Only four states of the non-South now leave it to local school authorities to determine whether or not school children shall be separated by race. Arizona required segregation at the grade school level until 1951, when the law was amended to make it optional. Kansas permits segregation in the elementary schools of its largest cities and in the high school of only one—Kansas City. New Mexico allows the separation of white and Negro pupils, and Wyoming authorizes segregated facilities where there are fifteen or more Negro pupils. (There is no indication, however, that any Wyoming communities are exercising their option to segregate.) (See Chart 1.)

Of the remaining non-Southern states, eleven have no explicit legal provisions regarding segregation, while sixteen have laws specifically prohibiting it. Since the end of World War II three of the latter have moved affirmatively to end educational segregation within their borders. New Jersey included a strong anti-segregation provision in the new constitution adopted in 1947 and special legislation was passed to implement it; Indiana repealed its permissive segregation law in 1949 and substituted for it a statute outlawing racial distinctions in the public schools; Illinois, which had long required non-segregated education, strengthened the old law in 1949 by adding an effective penalty provision. The most important sanction—now employed by Illinois and New Jersey—is the withholding of state financial aid from any school district which maintains separate schools.

The trend toward educational integration in the non-South has by no means resulted solely from the passage of new state laws or local ordinances. Many communities which have long maintained separate schools have moved away from segregation voluntarily, and for a variety of immediate reasons. The great underlying cause, however, has been the general redefinition of minority rights which has occupied the nation since it took up arms against a racist enemy in World War II. This has been reflected in persistent pressure from Negroes, now organized as never before, and from human relations agencies, church and civic groups, and school administrators themselves. The threat of legal action has played a part, too, as has the economic fact that it is often cheaper to integrate than to provide new or improved facilties for a small group of Negro pupils. The press of the non-South has been a positive force in the process, for even the most conservative newspapers are now generally sympathetic to the Negro's demand for equal treatment.

The trend toward integration has not proceeded without incident, of course. The worst race riots the nation has known in recent years have taken place in the non-South, and while none of these has been directly related to educational integration they are indicative of the tensions in many communities which are bound to be reflected in the administration of the public schools.

In the late summer of 1953 field studies for this report were made in 25 communities which had recently made, or were in the process of making transition from segregation to integration in their public schools. These of necessity had to be in the non-South, since no Southern community has yet abandoned dual education at the public school level. The communities ranged in size from 8,500 to 3,600,000 and in geographic distribution from New Jersey to New Mexico. As the following sampling will indicate, the experiences reported were as varied as the communities themselves.

Tucson, Arizona, integrated its public schools in 1951 with noteworthy smoothness. Within a few days after Arizona amended its segregation law to place separation of the races on an optional basis, the Tucson school board, at the behest of the superintendent, announced that the dual system would be abandoned at the beginning of the next term. The city's substantial Mexican-American community had not been segregated for some years, but Negroes, who made up 6.1 per cent of the population, had been required to send their children to separate schools below the high school level.

School officials had been preparing for the move for some time and there was active support for it among leading church and civic groups. The school board went the whole way from the beginning; a call for white volunteers to teach in the mixed schools produced twice the necessary number and a Negro principal was accepted without protest by a mixed teaching staff. The superintendent summed up Tucson's experience this way:

We treated the program as a natural, democratic and right thing. The School Board, the administrative staff, and the community backed us up completely. I had expected some opposition, but I actually received far less than I anticipated.

In Tucson the records show that only about 15 pupils out of a total of over 20,000 were withdrawn from the public schools in protest against integration.

The new Arizona law produced a far more cautious approach in Phoenix, a larger city than Tucson but with only a slightly higher percentage of Negro population (6.6). Various organizations and agencies urged the Phoenix school authorities to integrate the Negro high school and the three Negro elementary schools, but the board took no action. The NAACP then brought suit and while the litigation was still in the process of appeal the high school board decided to move toward partial de-segregation in 1953, and the elementary school district followed suit. The Phoenix formula was to authorize Negro students to attend the high school nearest their homes, while still retaining Carver Negro High as an "open school" without regard to districting. The complete Negro staff was retained at Carver, and the board has announced that the high school would be kept in operation from two to five years even though there were empty classrooms. This arrangement was based on the assumption that stiffer competition with the whites in the mixed schools and pride in Carver's extra-curricular activities would prompt most Negro students to turn to it voluntarily. In one of the three elementary school districts, plans were made for initial integration through the third grade in 1953, with the tentative goal of complete integration by 1954-55. The other two districts had not acted at the time of the study. No plans for integrating faculties had been announced.

Evansville, Indiana, has substantially maintained its dual school system despite a 1949 Indiana statute making integration mandatory within five years. A city of 128,638, with a Negro population of 6.6 per cent, Evansville lies across the Ohio River from Kentucky and has a distinctly Southern orientation. The school board met the new law with the announcement that all pupils would be free to attend any school they chose during the five year grace period. "It is the thinking of the board," the official announcement said, ". . . that [this] would provide the people of our community with a choice and their own actions in the coming years will indicate the pattern our schools will follow in the future."

Only eighteen Negro children enrolled in formerly all-white schools when the new policy went into effect after a series of public meetings in the affected neighborhoods. Only one protest from white parents was recorded, and this was firmly rejected by the school board president. As of the 1952-53 term, approximately fifty Negroes were attending the six "integrated" elementary schools; this represented only 4 per cent of the total Negro elementary enrollment, and a projection of the trend indicates that if all factors remain constant the total will be only 7.5 per cent at the end of the test period. Only one Negro had transferred from Lincoln High. He was well received in the white high school of his choice, as were the Negro children in the lower grades.

There has been no move to integrate school faculties in Evansville, nor has there been any particular necessity for it since the dual school system has continued virtually intact under the new policy.

Cincinnati, Ohio, like Evansville, is a "northern city with a Southern exposure." A heavy percentage of its half-million residents migrated across the Ohio River from the South, and about one-sixth of them are Negroes. Between 1940 and 1950, Cincinnati had a 44 per cent increase of Negro population, against only 6 per cent for the whites.

The official policy in Cincinnati has always been to maintain a single, integrated school system, but residential segregation practices have effectively split it into two wings. Within the past fifty years four schools were set up in the downtown Negro residential area, and while no pupils were specifically required to attend them all who did were—and are—Negroes. Segregation is not absolute, but 85 to 90 per cent of the Negro children go to schools where the student body is completely or predominantly Negro.

Cincinnati is now moving slowly toward a more integrated system through the requirement that all pupils who live within a district must attend the designated school regardless of race. The first four "districtings" produced no change at all, since they involved all-Negro neighborhoods, but the plan was to move on gradually to apply the policy to mixed neighborhoods. However, Cincinnati reversed the usual trend and pushed integration of faculties ahead of integration of pupils. In 1948 the first integrated faculty was organized in a school where 20 per cent of the pupils were white, and as of 1953 five elementary schools and two junior high schools maintained integrated faculties in fifty-fifty proportion.

The only incidents of disorder in connection with the transition to integration reported in the twenty-five communities surveyed occurred in Cairo, the southernmost city of Illinois lying at the confluence of the Mississippi and Ohio Rivers. This is hardly surprising since the history of the old river town often has been marked by violence, corruption, and in recent years, economic blight. Cairo's 1950 population of 12,123 represented a decrease of 16 per cent since 1940, and before the advent of the new atomic energy plants in nearby Kentucky many of its residents openly described it as "a dying city."

Cairo, where Negroes comprise one-third of the population, was one of a number of southern Illinois cities which had always completely ignored the 1874 statute banning

segregation in the public schools. Then in 1951 the legislature put teeth into the law by providing that no state funds
could be disbursed to any local school system until an official
of the school board had certified that the integration law was
being observed. State money, which is essential to the operation of the Cairo schools, was withheld briefly in 1951, and
the school board then contended that Cairo's obvious segregation was voluntary and that its official policy had always
been to permit any child to attend the school of his choice.
The superintendent pointed to the absence of applications
for transfer by Negroes as proof of the contention, and the
vital state funds were finally released.

On January 15, 1952, representatives of the NAACP called
upon the Cairo Board of Education to publicly state its admission policy. The Board declined, but indicated that applications from Negroes who wanted to transfer to white schools
would be accepted if they were made voluntarily. By January
25, requests for the transfer of 85 Negro pupils had been
filed. On the Friday before the opening of the new term,
however, the superintendent announced that more time
would be required to process the transfers and directed all
Negro pupils to report to separate schools as usual on Mon-
day. On opening day some Negroes defiantly took their children to the white schools for which they had applied, but
all were turned away.

Briefly, there was violence in Cairo—although no blood
was shed. Crosses were burned, shots were fired into the
homes of two local Negro leaders, and a charge of dynamite
was exploded outside the home of a Negro physician—who,
incidentally, had taken no part in the school-integration
effort. Local law enforcement agencies, backed by state
police and the FBI, moved promptly and order was quickly
restored and effectively maintained.

Many of the original Negro applicants withdrew in the

face of this outbreak, but by the end of the semester seventeen Negro children were enrolled in formerly segregated schools—ten in elementary schools and seven in junior and senior high schools. Since then the number has slowly increased until in June, 1953, it stood at sixty Negro pupils. No move has been made to integrate the faculties of the Cairo schools and apparently there are no plans to do so.

Like Illinois, New Jersey has long had a statute outlawing segregation in the public schools, but until the provision was incorporated in a new state constitution adopted in 1947 it was often observed only in the breach—particularly in the ten southernmost counties which have been described as "the Georgia of the North." As late as 1940 a study by Dr. Marion T. Wright recorded almost every conceivable form of racial relationship in the schools of the state:

These practices vary from the complete segregation of [Negro] children in the elementary schools of some of the southern counties of the state to situations in certain of the northern counties where there is complete integration of Negro children in the regular schools, which are staffed with teachers appointed according to merit and without regard to their racial identity. Between these two extremes there exist varying combinations of segregation and integration, such as: separate elementary schools and integrated junior and senior high schools; separate elementary and junior high schools and mixed high schools; divided buildings, one-half for Negroes and one-half for whites; separate classes and teachers for each race within the same building; separate elementary schools for each race on the same site; separate elementary schools joined by a common auditorium. In some instances, the Negro children are taught by Negro teachers in the regular subjects and by white teachers in the special subjects.

The new ban on segregation provided for the withholding of state funds from districts which did not comply, but the sanction had little practical meaning since most New Jersey school districts, unlike those of Illinois, depend primarily on local tax support. The job of enforcing the de-segregation policy fell to a new Division Against Discrimination created in the Department of Education to implement the new constitutional provisions. From the beginning it has relied primarily on persuasion. In 1948 there were 52 school districts containing one or more all-Negro schools with all-Negro faculties, and the division rated only nine of these the product of natural geographical factors. The separate schools in the other forty-three districts were attributed to deliberate segregation policies.

By the opening of the next school term thirty of the forty-three segregated districts had announced new policies of complete integration. Most of the other districts held out only for another term or two to adjust to their building programs. At the beginning of 1954 three districts were still operating segregated schools, but in all of these the Division Against Discrimination reported progress. Integration of faculties has generally kept pace with integration of students.

The foregoing by no means represents the full range of experience of the non-South in shaping its system of public education to meet the comparatively recent tides of Negro immigration. The samples cited here are those in which communities have recently made or begun the transition from segregation to integration; there are some where segregation has never been practiced, and others where it has been allowed to grow up unchecked. All these drastically condensed case histories can do is indicate some of the basic trends at work in the public schools of the non-South.

CHAPTER EIGHT

The Patterns of Transition

EDUCATIONAL SEGREGATION IS OBVIOUSLY THE PRODUCT OF racial attitudes, yet in the non-South there appears to be no fixed correlation between attitudes and geography or cultural and economic background. The most conspicuous generalization sustained by the case studies made for this report is that segregated schools are now principally the product of a larger pattern of separation of the races.

It is inevitable that residential segregation should produce segregation in education. This properly can be described as a natural process; any child normally attends the school nearest his home, and if he lives in an all-Negro neighborhood he is likely to attend an all-Negro school. And, since residential segregation of Negroes is still the prevailing pattern in the non-South, it also follows that the great majority of Negro children still attend predominantly Negro schools. The exceptions are the children of the few Negroes who have settled in rural areas or small towns, and those who live in the sections of the great cities where Negro residential sections merge with white neighborhoods in a constantly shifting pattern.

In his emigration from the South the Negro has become a city-dweller, and his dwelling-place is most often in the decaying heart of a metropolis. Chicago provides a classic example. The great waves of immigration in the wake of the two World Wars have increased the city's Negro population from 30,150 in 1900 to 492,267 in 1950, when it accounted for 13.6 per cent of the total. More than 90 per cent of these Negroes are jammed into eleven square miles of the South Side of Chicago, and in their efforts to break out of their ghetto they have encountered resistance all the way up the scale to the recent race riots in the suburb of Cicero.

In Chicago it can be demonstrated that segregated housing has not only made for segregated education, but for inferior education. The schools in or near the Negro neighborhoods are the oldest in the entire system, and provide the least adequate physical facilities. As slums always do, regardless of the race of their occupants, these depressed areas produce a high proportion of juvenile delinquents for the courts and "problem children" for the school system. Teaching jobs in such schools are obviously the least desirable from any standpoint, and the better qualified members of their faculties tend to flee as soon as the chronic teacher shortage opens up opportunities elsewhere. Thus the quality of instruction sags to the low level of the physical facilities, and every aspect of school operation is blighted by the depressed atmosphere of the surrounding communities. When students are lifted out of this background and "integrated" into more favored institutions it is not surprising that they often have difficulty making scholastic and social adjustments. The recognition that this is so provides one of the standard arguments for maintaining separate schools—and sets up a circle in which residential segregation creates a slum atmosphere, which reinforces the race prejudice of the community at large, which in turn is translated into the public attitudes which insist upon residential segregation.

These are the factors which have led some advocates of educational integration to argue their case not so much upon the ground of simple justice or of general improvement of educational opportunity, but as a matter of basic social reform. It is their thesis that a deliberate policy of integrating the schools is a necessary adjunct to rooting out race prejudice in any community. This line has met resistance from some educators who reply that they are being asked to divert their efforts from their primary mission. Dr. N. G. Fawcett, the superintendent of schools in Columbus, Ohio, has put it this way:

If integration of races is a by-product of establishing better schools, then we shall have integration of races. I can see no good reason for drawing district lines just to create integration any more than to create segregation.

This issue is not likely to be resolved soon, but those on both sides can agree that segregation in education in the non-South will not be eliminated so long as rigidly segregated residential patterns survive. Stronger laws more vigorously enforced, and firmer administrative policies more sympathetically applied, have had and will have a profound effect upon bi-racial education—but they are aimed only at a single symptom of a basic community relationship.

This has been reflected in the variety of administrative techniques adopted by those cities which have been called upon to effect educational integration under permissive or mandatory state laws. In general, communities where the Negro population is small and where inter-racial relationships are good have tended to go the whole way at a stroke, as in Tucson. In every instance of this kind reported, the transition was rated a complete success—but it must also be noted that these were cities where the small proportion of Negro population prevented residential patterns from becoming a determinant.

Most communities have proceeded more cautiously, undertaking to integrate the schools by gradual stages. Some have started at the top; one New Mexican community began by integrating grades nine through twelve. Others have started at the bottom, as in Phoenix where integration in the elementary schools was first undertaken from the kindergarten through the third grade. Most Indiana communities have exercised the option in the 1949 state law, which allows a five-year transition period, and are moving, as in Evansville, on a more or less voluntary basis.

The usual reason given for the gradual approach is the fear of adverse public reaction, but there are other considerations that undoubtedly weigh heavily with school boards and administrators. Uncertainty as to the ability of Negroes to hold their own in mixed schools because of generally inferior educational and cultural backgrounds is often advanced as a deterrent. And those officials who are hesitant to assign Negroes to teach white students face practical problems of teacher tenure. The simplest way to avoid the issue is to postpone the dissolution of all-Negro schools.

The ultimate in delayed integration is achieved in those communities which maintain segregated schools within an officially integrated educational system. Cincinnati, for instance, has maintained separate schools for 50 years under a stated policy which does not recognize their existence. In many of these communities, school officials operate on the theory that when a choice is provided most Negroes will elect to remain in segregated schools. Experience thus far has tended to bear them out, although it is not clear whether this reflects the real desires of Negro patrons or only inertia bolstered by the tacit official disapproval of integration evidenced in the adoption of such a policy.

Proponents of the gradual approach argue that it minimizes public resistance to integration. But some school officials who have experienced it believe the reverse is true. A markedly gradual program, they contend, particularly one which involves the continued maintenance of some separate schools, invites opposition and allows time for it to be organized. Whatever the merit of this argument, the case histories clearly indicate a tendency for local political pressure to be applied by both sides when the question of integration is raised, and when policies remain unsettled for a protracted period the pressures mount. One school board member in Arizona privately expressed the wish that the state had gone all the way and made integration mandatory instead of optional—thus giving the board something to point to as justification for its action.

There is also the practical consideration that partial integration is likely to intensify the scholastic handicaps of successive classes of Negro children, who receive their initial schooling in inferior segregated schools and then are thrown into direct competition with better-prepared whites.

The matter of integrating faculties is generally regarded as more of a problem than mixing classes. In community after community school authorities who had experienced no serious difficulty in admitting Negroes to formerly all-white schools expressed the fear that white patrons would not tolerate Negroes teaching their children.

Experience with integrated faculties, however, is far from negative. Although there are exceptions, most white teachers have tended to take a professional view of the matter and subordinate any adverse personal reaction they may have had. For entirely different reasons, it appears that there has been at least as much tacit opposition to the move on the part of Negro teachers who are afraid of losing their jobs through discrimination or direct competition with better-trained whites.

Protests from parents against integrated faculties have been common, but they have tended to diminish and even to disappear as the experience is continued. Those communities which experienced the least friction in the course of transition generally made a careful selection of teachers to serve as members of the first mixed faculties, and also saw to it that advance explanation was made to parents of both races. Some administrators have met initial objections with assurances that transfers would be granted to teachers or pupils if they were dissatisfied after a reasonable trial period; in practice this has resulted in few transfers.

Many administrators report a remarkable change of heart on the part of those who initially objected to faculty integration after they had had personal experiences with it. In one community the local PTA requested that an especially popular Negro teacher be rotated among the remaining all-white schools of the city so that all could share in this inter-racial experience. And in some cases the reluctant Negro faculty members have found that the demand for trained teachers has been sufficient to offset any tendency toward discrimination against them. In New Jersey 415 of the state's 479 Negro teachers were employed in the nine counties that maintained segregated schools in 1945. The most recent record indicates that 425 Negro teachers are still employed in those counties under integration, while the statewide total has risen to 645.

The most important factor in integration of the public schools in the non-South, finally, is community attitudes. It is axiomatic that separate schools can be merged only with great difficulty, if at all, when a great majority of the citizens.

who support them are actively opposed to the move. No
other public activity is so closely identified with local mores.
Interest in the schools is universal, and it is an interest
that directly involves not only the tax-payer but his family,
and therefore his emotions. Those who are indifferent to all
other community affairs tend to take a proprietary interest
in the schools their children attend, or will attend, or have
attended. State influence in public education has grown
in recent years in proportion to the increase in state aid,
but state policies rarely are so important as local forces in
the shaping of public educational policies and practices.

In the matter of racial segregation this has meant that
state laws and administrative policies often have been
ignored, avoided, or substantially modified by local school
authorities. Usually this has been done by officials who justified their action on the ground that they were reflecting the
prevailing sentiment of their communities. But the fact is
that for some years American attitudes in racial matters have
been in a state of flux, and not even a school administrator
who makes it his business to keep a sensitive finger on the
public pulse can be certain in advance how his community
will react to a specific situation. One thing that stands out in
these case histories is the frequency with which those who
have had experience with integration—professional educators
and laymen alike—have steeled themselves for a far more
severe public reaction than they actually encountered.

It is dangerous to generalize in these matters, and very
probably footless in view of the tremendous variety of American community life. One of the intangible factors involves
the distinction between *passive* and *active* resistance to
abandoning long-standing practices of segregation in the
schools, or at any other point of universal contact between
the races. The most meticulous house-to-house poll in any
American community with a sizeable Negro population

would doubtless turn up a negative response to a proposal to integrate the separate public schools. In the case of the whites this might reflect deep-seated race prejudice, or it might be no more than the normal, instinctive resistance to any marked change in the accustomed patterns of everyday living. In many cases the basis of objection might be the demonstrable fact that the great majority of American Negroes are still slum-dwellers; many a parent who proudly considers himself wholly tolerant in racial matters will object to having his child associate with classmates of inferior economic and social background. It is probable that some resistance to integration would even be recorded among Negroes, who might respond negatively out of simple fear of the unknown, or the desire to protect their children against possible overt discrimination by white classmates or teachers. The great problem for schoolmen who have been moved to consider integration by their own convictions, or by the prodding of higher authority, has been to determine whether the passive resistance which they can readily sense will be translated into active resistance once the issue is drawn. In any event the superintendent who is called to take his school system from segregation to integration must be prepared to function as a "social engineer." He will deal on a mass scale with delicate problems of human relationships involving not only pupils and teachers but the community at large.

These case studies demonstrate that wherever there has been an active and well-planned program to "sell" integration to the community at large it has succeeded—but here again there is no way to measure just how difficult the selling job really was. The most notable examples are to be found in New Jersey, where a well-staffed state agency made it its business to work closely with those communities which had long practiced segregation and appeared resistant to the change required by the new constitution. Although New

Jersey's Division Against Discrimination was armed with the power to withhold state funds and even to bring misdemeanor charges against school officials who refused to comply, it accomplished the integration of forty formerly segregated school districts without invoking these powers in a single instance.

At the other end of the scale is Cairo, Illinois, where the effort of the NAACP to force a reluctant school board to accept the state ban on segregation led to violence. Cairo, in almost every aspect of its community life, may be classified as a "sick city," and there is no indication of anything approximating an orderly inter-racial approach to the problem either before or after integration became an explosive issue.

Between these two extremes lie most of the non-Southern cities. They are, for the most part, beyond the reach of any possible decision of the Supreme Court in the test cases, for segregation in the schools of the non-South is now rarely bolstered by law, and where it is it would hardly miss the legal prop if it were struck down. De-segregation is proceeding there at a rate determined by the willingness of individual communities to accept the change—or by the willingness of community leaders to put the issue to the test.

CHAPTER NINE

The Nation's Capital: A Special Case

THE LEGAL, SOCIAL, AND ECONOMIC FORCES THAT ARE RE-shaping the nation's bi-racial educational structure can perhaps best be seen in a detailed examination of the educational problems of an American city that in many ways is atypical. To most persons in this country and abroad Washington is more an institution than a city, a symbol rather than a community. Yet some 800,000 people live in the nation's capital; they earn their living there, raise their families, and educate their children and if they are, for the most part, rootless this gives the city a special significance as the place where America's regional attitudes meet and merge.

Washington houses the nation's government, but it has no government of its own. Its citizens, if they can be called that, elect none of their local officials, have no representation in the federal government, and cannot even vote for the president who heads the federal community. Their domain is a tiny enclave surrounded by the sovereign states of Maryland and Virginia and no intermediate level of government exists between them and the Congress of the United States, of which they are the often neglected wards. Executive functions are performed by three commissioners of the

District of Columbia—two civilians appointed by the president, and one officer of the Army Engineer Corps. The Congress itself acts in lieu of a city council in legislative matters. Funds for the support of the municipal government are appropriated annually as a part of the federal budget. There are some municipal boards that in practice are wholly independent, but at the same time departments of the national government exercise direct control in some local affairs.

Basically, Washington is a white-collar city. It has no industries of consequence, and its commerce is self-contained. It is a cosmopolitan community by virtue of the embassies and legations of foreign nations which are concentrated there, but it received few of the European immigrants who flocked to the United States in successive waves after the Civil War. The migrants who have formed a great city around the hard core of native Washingtonians were already Americans and they came from every section of the country, North, East, South, and West. Most of them were attracted by jobs in the government bureaus, which have multiplied like amoebae in the wake of the New Deal, World War II, and the Cold War; some spend only a few years in the capital without anticipation of permanent residence, but many decide to live out their days in the pleasant, tree-shaded city.

After emancipation Washington became the first great Mecca for the freed slaves, and today Negroes make up a third of the District's population—a percentage higher than that of most Southern cities. Nearly a fourth of Washington's Negroes are in the white-collar class, largely by virtue of long-standing if imperfectly implemented policies against discrimination in federal employment. But the city also has an unusually large number of Negro doctors, lawyers, and other self-employed professionals.

As a result, the economic status of Washington's Negro community ranks it near the top among comparable concentrations of Negro population. Yet it is still at the bottom of the city's income scale. Some 14 per cent of the employed Negroes are laborers, 13 per cent are in private domestic service, and 25 per cent are employed in the service trades. In 1950, 43 per cent of Washington's non-white families had annual incomes of less than $2,000, against 24 per cent for the white population. Negroes comprise 60 per cent of the city's slum-dwellers.

In the 1940's the capital experienced unprecedented expansion as the war brought in thousands of new federal job-holders. Like all American cities, Washington spread out into brand-new suburbs, but unlike most of the others its outskirts soon stretched across two state lines. The new satellite communities outside the District are almost entirely white, which has resulted in a sharp rise in the percentage of Negro population in what is still officially the city of Washington—from 28 per cent of the total in 1940 to 35 per cent in 1950. Moreover the white families who trekked from the central sections to the Maryland and Virginia suburbs included a high proportion of those with school-age children, which sent Negro enrollment in the Washington school system upward from 38 per cent of the total in 1940 to 51 per cent in 1950, the highest proportion in any American city of more than 100,000 population.

Perhaps because the Negro migration began earlier and was more gradual than in most non-Southern communities, and because there has never been a heavy concentration of foreign-born residents, Washington never developed the clearly-defined "ghetto" pattern that marks New York, Chicago, and other major non-Southern centers. The Negro population originally concentrated in the central northwest and far northeast areas, but the Negro sections were never rigidly demarcated. In recent years Negroes have sought to escape the poor housing in the downtown areas by moving into the homes and apartments vacated by white families in the great exodus to the suburbs, and racially mixed neighborhoods have been on the increase. The National Capital Housing Authority has recently established a non-segregation policy, with the result that 93 per cent of Washington's public housing projects have been opened to both races.

All told, Washington probably has less residential segregation than any American city with a sizeable Negro population, and yet through most of its history it has maintained most of the other racial barriers common to the region that extends southward across the Potomac. The only notable concessions to equality for Negroes until recent years were in federal employment, public transportation, and public buildings. Theaters, hotels, restaurants, and recreation areas maintained a rigid color bar. This reflected both the Southern outlook of the original city, and the political fact that Southerners tended to gain senior positions on the committees of Congress which determine the policies to be observed in the capital city.

Yet always Washington has been particularly sensitive to the forces that have been working against segregation. When the Daughters of the American Revolution refused to allow Marian Anderson to sing in Constitution Hall because she happened to be a Negro, no less a personage than the first lady of the land stepped forward to protest—and what would have been no more than a local incident in any other American city became a matter of moment all over the world. Both major political parties having declared against racial segregation, their leaders can hardly ignore examples of discrimination that turn up under their noses as they go about the business of governing the nation. And in the post-World War II era a powerful international force has been added to the domestic pressures against segregation, with Washington as its natural focus.

The Communist world has made racial segregation in the United States a prime issue in the propaganda campaigns that have marked the progress of the Cold War since 1946. The great prizes are Asia and the Middle-East whose nations for the most part remain uncommitted in the struggle between East and West. Communist propagandists have skillfully played upon the sensibilities of the brown and yellow peoples of those areas, arguing that a nation which discriminates against its own dark-skinned citizens can never be trusted with the leadership of Asians or Moslems. And they have succeeded, at least to the point that a minor racial incident in Selma, Alabama, is likely to rate more space on the front page of a Bombay newspaper than the most incisive attack upon the Communist terror by an American delegate to the United Nations. The makers of American foreign policy have viewed this tendency with increasing alarm, which has not diminished under the transition from a Democratic to a Republican regime in Washington. The capital city, they have insisted, of all places must be above reproach in its treatment of racial minorities.

Under the added weight of this new pressure Washington's racial barriers recently have been eliminated in restaurants, and theaters, and somewhat diminished in hotel accommodations. The last citadel of absolute segregation is the Washington public school system.

Washington's schools are divided into two distinct wings —Division One for whites, and Division Two for Negroes. This segregated organization carries through all levels of the school program, from kindergarten through the teachers colleges, in special education, extra-curricular programs, and adult education. The administrative and supervisory staffs are divided with equal strictness. Only at the very top administrative level, where all positions are filled by white personnel, do the two divisions merge. Under the superintendent and his assistants a white staff serves Division One and a Negro staff Division Two.

Washington has shared with other American cities the severe dislocations of the post-war years, which saw school enrollment rise sharply, and the cost of expanding or replacing outmoded school buildings almost double. A study of the Washington school system by Dr. George D. Strayer in 1948-49 found nearly one-fourth of the school buildings then in use in such poor condition as not to justify expenditure for improvement. Well over half the buildings were rated as sub-standard, and of the nine rated as "very satisfactory" only one was in the Negro division. Thirty-five per cent of the white schools and 56 per cent of the Negro schools were more than 40 years old, and some were more than 70.

The age of the school buildings underscored Washington's peculiar problems, for in many respects its physical plant was located to serve a city that no longer existed. With population shifting at an unprecedented rate, the schools often were no longer where the children were. And segregation seriously complicated the problem for as formerly unmixed neighborhoods became interracial two schools were required where only one had been needed before. A recent annual report by the superintendent contained this summary statement:

The most difficult problems to solve are those relating to the shifting and changing nature of our population. These changes take place so rapidly that there is a serious resultant lack of facilities in some localities. The most difficult phase of this general problem is the changing ratio between school enrollment in Division One and Division Two. The declining enrollments in the schools of Division One and the rapidly increasing enrollment in Division Two are causing a serious imbalance between the two divisions in numbers of teachers and schoolhouse facilities.

By any measurement, the Negro division of the Washington school system has remained inferior to the white. In 1950-51, the last year for which a complete accounting is available, the expenditure per white pupil was $273.21 against $212.02 per Negro pupil. Strayer's study found 88.1 per cent of the Negro elementary classes above the desired maximum of 30 pupils, against 67.9 per cent for the whites; the corresponding figure for classes above 40 was 40.3 per cent for Negroes and 18 per cent for whites. In 1953-54 elementary schools classified as overcrowded house 38.2 per cent of the white children and 86 per cent of the Negroes. Negro junior high schools are short more than 1,200 seats. Yet the seven white senior high schools, all of which have high adequacy ratings, are now used only to 48.2 per cent of capacity.

In recent years the Negro schools in Washington have had difficulty providing enough teachers for the full organization of classes, even though more qualified Negro teachers have been certified each year than have been employed. The shortage results from the failure to allocate enough salary funds to the Negro division, even though the white division now has more teachers than Board standards require. The corporation counsel, who is chief legal officer for the system, has ruled that it would be illegal to transfer surplus white teachers to Negro schools.

The maintenance of the dual system in a city where residential segregation is rapidly breaking down causes an increasing number of children to travel long distances to school. In the interracial neighborhoods the districting of elementary schools has become meaningless, for if there is only one school one group or the other has to go outside the neighborhood for its schooling. The inconvenience has cut both ways. For example, the new River Terrace Elementary School was originally intended for whites, but by the time it was completed there was a greater need for Negro classrooms in the mixed neighborhood in which it is located, with the result that white children now have to cross a major highway to attend the inferior Benning School. The problem of travel is most severe for Negroes at the high school level, who have to travel as far as six miles to reach one of the three Negro institutions.

The continuing effort to superimpose a rigidly segregated school system upon a rapidly shifting residential pattern has made crises, financial and otherwise, the norm in the Washington school system. The direct dollar and cents cost of maintaining segregation was estimated in 1952 by the then Commissioner F. Joseph Donohue as between seven and eight million dollars annually—more than one-fourth of the entire school budget.

There has also been a high cost in terms of community-wide frustration and tension. The effort to preserve the uncertain balance between the white and Negro divisions has often involved transferring facilities from the use by one race to the other. This might work if affected neighborhoods changed character quickly and became all white or all Negro. The fact is that they do not, and a neighborhood usually changes character gradually until it reaches the point that the white school is not wholly empty but half-empty. Negro and white parents are then placed in competition for the most convenient school facilities for their children and bitter racial controversy is a frequent result.

Inevitably the Washington school system has become the subject of legal attack. The Board of Education and the Corporation Counsel have held that while the laws of Congress have never specifically made segregation mandatory, they have assumed complete separation of the races in the Washington schools. This interpretation is challenged in the case of *Bolling* v. *Sharpe* which is now before the Supreme Court. One effect of this action has been to open up for the first time general public discussion of the possibility of integrating the schools.

The school board has solicited and received the recommendations of many community organizations on the best way of integrating the dual system if the Court should so order—limiting its hearings to the *means* of integration so as to avoid any debate on its desirability. The participating organizations represented viewpoints ranging from resigned acceptance of a plainly distasteful possibility to militant advocacy of integration. There was general agreement on three points: that if it came integration should be initiated by a firm policy; that as a part of the transition white and Negro pupils should be assigned to schools on a residential basis; and that teachers should be hired on the basis of competitive examination without regard to race. On other points there was a considerable divergence of opinion, principally stemming from the question of whether integration should be immediate and complete throughout the system, or whether it should be carried out gradually. The school board has officially indicated that it favors a gradual approach.

While the immediate future of bi-racial education in Washington apparently hinges on the action of the Supreme Court, the peculiar nature of the city's governmental structure and of its symbolic importance as the nation's capital means that the dual school system cannot escape sustained pressure no matter what the Court may do. At any time Congress could end segregation by the passage of a simple resolution. Nobody who lives there doubts that sooner or later Washington will find out how good a prophet Judge Edgerton was when he wrote in his dissenting opinion in the *Carr* case of 1950:

It is sometimes suggested that the due process of law cannot require what law cannot enforce. No such suggestion is relevant here. When United States courts order integration of District of Columbia schools, they will be integrated. It has been too long forgotten that the District of Columbia is not a provincial community but the cosmopolitan capital of a nation that professes democracy.

CHAPTER TEN

Plessy Comes Back to Court

IN 1952 THE LONG COURSE OF LITIGATION WHICH BEGAN WHEN Charles Sumner appeared in court in Boston in 1849 brought before the United States Supreme Court five cases in which the *Plessy* doctrine was directly challenged. In all but one of these the Negro plaintiffs were represented by attorneys for the National Association for the Advancement of Colored People, which had made it quite clear that its interests range far beyond the legal matters at hand. In a press release the NAACP thus summed up its position:

At ultimate stake is the future of the anachronistic system of segregation not only in education but also in all other phases of public life in the nation. We of the NAACP have long maintained that segregation is a divisive and anti-democratic device designed to perpetuate an obsolete caste system which flatly contravenes the basic ethical concepts of our Judaeo-Christian tradition. We have held that segregation *per se* is unconstitutional. Should the Court uphold this point of view it could mean that all laws requiring or permitting racial segregation in schools, transportation, recreation, shelter, and public accommodations generally would ultimately be invalid.

When Thurgood Marshall and the other NAACP lawyers associated with him address the nine justices of the country's highest tribunal . . . they will contend, at least by implication, that integration cannot be a half-way measure. Our nation cannot remain half-integrated and half-segregated today any more than it could continue half-free and half-slave a century ago.

This echo of the ancient debates of the abolitionist era had drawn a reply in kind from the South. Governor James F. Byrnes of South Carolina, himself a former associate justice of the Supreme Court, said in an address to the South Carolina Education Association:

Every child in the state, white or colored, should have the opportunity for a full public school education. It must be our goal to see that each of them accepts that opportunity. . . .

My hope is that the record to be considered by [the Supreme Court] will show that regardless of how we may have failed in the past to provide substantially equal facilities, that a courageous and forward-looking legislature has enacted a law providing an educational program that will improve facilities for Negro children as well as for white children. I hope too it can show that the governor of this state has said he will use what influence he has to accomplish that end. . . .

Should the Supreme Court decide this case against our position, we will face a serious problem. Of only one thing can we be certain. South Carolina will not now, nor for some years to come, mix white and colored children in our schools. . . . If the Court changes what is now the law of the land, we will, if it is possible, live within the law, preserve the public school system, and at the same time maintain segregation. If that is not possible, reluctantly we will abandon the public school system.

Alex McCullough, Governor Byrnes' secretary, later wrote of the address that the governor "seemed to indicate in that speech that he does not expect segregation in the schools to continue forever." But, as McCullough also noted, Byrnes had left no doubt as to his position for the present, and his stand had since been endorsed by Governor Herman Talmadge of Georgia, who had pushed a "preparedness program" through his legislature intended to permit his state to place the operation of its public schools in private hands if the Court should ban segregation.

It was against this background that the Supreme Court undertook consideration of the school cases before it. An imposing array of counsel twice argued the issues; the NAACP's highly-skilled staff headed the legal battery for the plaintiffs, and on the other side South Carolina bolstered the skills of the various state attorneys general by retaining as its principal spokesman the noted New York corporation lawyer and one-time Democratic presidential nominee, John W. Davis. In addition two briefs were filed by the Department of Justice, one before the Democrats left office and another in the name of the present Republican attorney general. In both the federal government generally lined up on the side of the plaintiffs.

It was inevitable that these cases should receive special attention from the Court and from the public. The immediate issue was the constitutionality of segregation in the public schools of the United States; the implications, as the NAACP noted, touched upon the whole of the nation's segregated society, and, as the defense stressed, upon the basic structure of the republic as it involves the division of authority between the federal government and the sovereign states. There were moral overtones, too, and they had their practical consequence in terms of an American foreign policy that sought to keep the brown and yellow peoples of the world from swinging into the Communist orbit.

The brief filed in the name of the Democratic U. S. Attorney General in December, 1952, was addressed directly to this point:

It is in the context of the present world struggle between freedom and tyranny that the problem of racial discrimination must be viewed. . . . The existence of discrimination against minority groups in the United States has an adverse effect upon our relations with other countries. Racial discrimination furnishes grist for the Communist propaganda mills, and it raises doubt even among friendly nations as to the intensity of our devotion to the democratic faith.

In this brief the Attorney General also introduced the expert testimony of the Secretary of State:

In response to a request from the Attorney General, the Secretary of State wrote, in part: "As might be expected, Soviet spokesmen regularly exploit [racial discrimination] in propaganda against the United States, both within the United Nations and through radio broadcasts and the press, which reaches all corners of the world. . . . The segregation of school children on a racial basis is one of the practices in the United States which has been singled out for hostile foreign comment in the United Nations and elsewhere. Other peoples cannot understand how such a practice can exist in a country which professes to be a staunch supporter of freedom, justice and democracy. The sincerity of the United States in this respect will be judged by its deeds as well as by its words."

The course of litigation was understandably slow. Most of these cases were many months old when they were first argued before the Supreme Court in December, 1952. Yet a year later the Court was still engaged in hearing another round of written and oral argument offered at its specific request.

The Court's ruling might very well establish a new legal doctrine, but it would have to be cast in terms of the specific cases before it. Each of these cases raised the basic issue in a somewhat different way. They were:

Clarendon County, South Carolina (Briggs v. Elliot)

In June of 1951, forty Negro parents asked a special three-judge federal court to order an end to segregation as prescribed by state law in the schools of their district. The NAACP attorneys who represented them argued that the state law violates the Fourteenth Amendment, and that it has resulted in gross inequalities in the school facilities available to the children of this low-country South Carolina county.

With one judge dissenting (J. Waties Waring of Charleston, now retired, whose rulings in other cases involving the rights of Negroes have made him a highly controversial figure in the state) the court held the South Carolina segregation law constitutional, but found that the school facilities provided for the two races were substantially unequal. School authorities were directed to launch an equalization program and report back to the court in six months on their progress.

The case was immediately appealed to the Supreme Court, but by the time it was heard the six-months period had elapsed. The Supreme Court remanded the case, directing the lower court to consider the district's progress report and take whatever action it deemed appropriate. On March 13, 1952, the district court held that satisfactory progress toward equalization was being made and that it therefore saw no reason to alter its original ruling. The plaintiffs conceded that facilities were being equalized but renewed their appeal to the Supreme Court solely on the issue of segregation.

Prince Edward County, Virginia (Davis v. County School Board)

The litigation here involved the appeal by a group of Negroes for admission of their children to the county's white high school. Alternatively, they asked that certain inequalities in high school facilities be removed. As in Clarendon, a three-judge federal court upheld the state segregation law but found that the existing facilities were in fact unequal. The court ordered the school board to "pursue with diligence and dispatch their present progress, now afoot and progressing, to replace the Moton (Negro high school) buildings and facilities with a new building and new equipment, or otherwise to remove the inequalities in them." On appeal the plaintiffs asked the Supreme Court to overrule the lower court and order their children admitted to the white high school.

Topeka, Kansas (Brown v. Board of Education)

On the authority of state law, Topeka segregated white and Negro pupils in the first six grades. Negro parents charged in federal court that this practice denied their children their constitutional right of "equal protection of the laws." The plaintiffs conceded that the school facilities and services provided for the two races were substantially equal, but the NAACP attorneys brought in a battery of social scientists to testify that segregation imposed serious social and psychological handicaps upon the Negro children. The three-judge Court accepted this thesis, saying in its decision that "segregation with the sanction of law . . . has a tendency to retard the educational and mental development of Negro children." But this finding of fact did not lead the court to declare segregation unconstitutional; it considered itself bound by previous U. S. Supreme Court precedent to uphold segregation in the absence of any demonstrable inequalities in the dual system.

Appeal was duly filed in the Topeka case, but in the meantime the Topeka Board of Education voted "to terminate the maintenance of segregation in the elementary grades as rapidly as possible." This may have had the effect of rendering the case moot—that is, no longer presenting an issue.

Wilmington, Delaware (Belton v. Gebhart, Bulah v. Gebhart)

In both these suits a Delaware state court was requested to order Negro children admitted to the nearest white school. The local court found substantial inequality in the facilities available, and, while noting that only the Supreme Court could overturn the *Plessy* precedent, held that segregation in this instance served to deprive the plaintiffs of equal educational opportunity. The court's remedy was to order the Negro children admitted to the white school until such time as the Negro schools were brought up to parity, and the decision was upheld by the Delaware Supreme Court, although it based its decision solely on inequality, and explicitly refrained from treating the question of segregation as such.

The Delaware decision differed significantly from the Virginia and South Carolina cases, in that it declared the right of plaintiffs to equal facilities to be present and personal. In effect the court made the point that a child seeking relief would be denied a certain part of his education if he were forced to wait until physical facilities were equalized, and interpreted *Plessy* to mean that schools could be "separate if *now* equal." The basis of the appeal of school authorities to the Supreme Court was that the Delaware courts had not allowed a reasonable time for equalization, as in the federal cases.

Washington, District of Columbia (Bolling v. Sharpe)

Different points of law from those raised in the other cases were involved here because the school system in question operates directly under the federal government. The litigation was based primarily on the Fifth Amendment, rather than the Fourteenth. The plaintiffs charged that Negro children were unlawfully excluded from Sousa Junior High School solely because of their race. They maintained that nothing in the statutes of the District of Columbia, as enacted by Congress, empowers the Board of Education to operate separate schools for Negroes and whites. The defense argued that by the language of its appropriation acts the Congress has consistently recognized and approved segregation in the District schools. The federal district court granted a defense motion to dismiss the suit on the ground that the issue of inequality of facilities had not been raised. The Supreme Court was asked to reverse the lower court's dismissal of the case and rule on the constitutional issue.

It will be seen from these brief summaries that without exception the lower courts accepted "separate but equal" as their guiding principle. Even in Kansas, where the Court agreed with the plaintiffs' contention that segregation is a deterrent to equality of educational opportunity, the judges felt themselves bound by U. S. Supreme Court precedent to hold equal, separate schools constitutional. And the Delaware courts, while ordering Negroes admitted to a white school, hedged their decision with the declaration that the constitutionality of segregation was not at issue. Thus, while the *Plessy* doctrine might have been shaken by this litigation it was still standing, and nothing short of a clear-cut decision by the Supreme Court could strike it down.

It was also evident that there was no common judicial agreement on the proper remedy for inequalities in a dual school system. In this respect, each of the five cases raised a different question. Could school authorities lawfully be permitted time to provide equal facilities? If so, how much time should they have? On the other hand, assuming that the plaintiffs have a personal and immediate right to relief, how long could they be required to wait for equalization? Where there was no issue but the constitutionality of segregation, was a lower court justified in dismissing the case?

The Supreme Court indicated that it had been pondering these and related matters ever since it agreed to joint consideration of the five cases. On June 8, 1953, in calling for further argument, the Court submitted a list of searching questions to opposing counsel.

In the first place, the Court wanted to know the views of the litigants on the genesis of the Fourteenth Amendment with reference to bi-racial education—whether or not the Congress which submitted the Fourteenth Amendment and the state legislatures and conventions which approved it understood that it would abolish segregation in the schools. At the December, 1953, hearing counsel for the plaintiffs argued firmly and eloquently that the end of segregation in education was clearly the intent of the framers of the amendment; with equal firmness and eloquence counsel for the defense argued that it was no such thing. The brief submitted on behalf of U. S. Attorney General Brownell rested on the middle ground established by the scholars who had inquired into the subject over the years:

... (1) that the primary and pervasive purpose of the Fourteenth Amendment, as is shown by its history and as has repeatedly been declared by this Court, was to secure for Negroes full and complete equality before the law and to abolish all legal distinctions based on race or color; (2) that the legislative history of the Amendment in Congress is not conclusive; (3) that the available materials relating to the ratification proceedings in the various state legislatures are too scanty and incomplete, and the specific references to school segregation too few and scattered, to justify any definite conclusion as to the existence of a general understanding in such legislatures as to the effect which the Amendment would have on school segregation. . . .

The Court also raised a question as to whether the Congress might in the exercise of the power granted it by the Fourteenth Amendment move to abolish segregation in public education, and whether the judicial power might be used to the same end. This was familiar ground, which had been battled over many times since the issue of segregation in education was first brought to law. The plaintiffs contended that the Court does have such power, and the briefs submitted by two United States attorneys general concurred. The defendants insisted that the state legislatures are the proper bodies to determine the racial pattern of education, and that the Court itself has recognized this since the *Plessy* doctrine was propounded in 1896. This, of course, was the fundamental issue before the Court; in choosing between these two positions it would decide whether or not segregated schools could be continued under the sanction of federal law.

Beyond the basic constitutional arguments, the Court also dealt in its list of questions with the possible implementation of a decision against segregation. Could the Court, in the exercise of its equity powers, permit a gradual transition from segregated to integrated schools?

The then attorney general, who argued for the end of segregation in the 1952 brief, urged that the Court not only could but should allow for "an orderly and expeditious transfer to a non-segregated system." The brief said:

The fact that a system or practice is determined to be unlawful does not of itself require the Court to order that it be abandoned forthwith. A reasonable period of time will obviously be required to permit formulation of new provisions of law governing the administration of schools in areas affected by the Court's decision. School authorities may wish to give pupils a choice of attending one of several schools, a choice now prohibited. Teachers may have to be transferred, and teaching schedules rearranged....

These are indicative of the kinds of problems that may arise in giving effect to a holding that separate but equal school systems are unconstitutional. We suggest that any relief which this Court may direct should contemplate the possibility of such problems and afford opportunity for their expeditious settlement within a specified period. Moreover, to the extent that there may exist popular opposition in some sections to abolition of racially-segregated school systems, we believe that a program for orderly and progressive transition would tend to lessen such antagonism.

In its fifth question, the Court queried the attorneys as to their ideas of what legal devices might be employed to effect "gradual adjustment to non-segregation." The Court wanted to know whether it should formulate detailed decrees, whether it should appoint a special master to hear further evidence with a view to shaping special orders in each case, or whether it should remand the cases to the lower courts with general directions under which they could frame decrees of their own.

The Brownell brief—which the Attorney General's representative conceded in oral argument departed in no way from the principles set forth under the previous administration—discussed in some detail proposed mechanics for transition:

1. That racial segregation in public schools be decreed by this court to be a violation of the rights secured by the Constitution;

2. That each case be remanded to the appropriate court of first instance for such further proceedings and orders as are necessary and proper to carry out the Court's decision;

3. That the lower courts be directed on remand to enter decrees under which the defendants shall forthwith be enjoined from using race or color as a basis for determining admission of children to public schools under their authority or control; provided, however, that if the defendants show that it is impracticable or inequitable to grant the plaintiffs the remedy of immedi-

ate (*i.e.*, at the beginning of the next school term) admission to nonsegregated schools, the court shall order the defendants to propose and, on approval by the court after a public hearing, to put into effective operation a program for transition to a nonsegregated school system as expeditiously as the circumstances permit;

4. That for the accomplishment of these purposes, taking into view the difficulties which may be encountered, a period of one year be allowed from the receipt of this Court's mandate, with leave, however, in the event, in the judgment of the lower court, the necessities of the situation so require, to extend such period for a further reasonable time; and that, in the event before the expiration of the period thus fixed, a condition in harmony with the requirements of the Constitution is not brought about, it shall be the duty of the lower court to enter appropriate orders, by way of injunction or otherwise, directing immediate admission of the plaintiffs to nonsegregated schools; and

5. That this Court retain jurisdiction for the purpose of making such further orders and decrees, if any, as may become necessary for carrying out its mandate.

Despite the cautious approach suggested in the convolutions of 3 and 4, all of the litigants showed a notable lack of enthusiasm for gradualism. In its brief offered in response to the Court's questions, the NAACP said: "In accordance with instructions of this Court we have addressed ourselves to all the plans for gradual adjustment which we have been able to find. None would be effective." And in oral argument John W. Davis said, " . . . we find nothing here on which this Court could formulate a decree, nor do we think the court below has any power to formulate a decree, reciting in what manner these schools are to be altered at all, and what course the State of South Carolina shall take concerning it. Your Honors do not sit, and cannot sit as a glorified board of education for the State of South Carolina or any other state. Neither can the district court."

Whether the Court's written questions, or its extended

interrogation of counsel upon re-argument, could be taken as indicating the trend of thought among the nine justices was debatable. But the manner in which the Court proceeded with this litigation made it clear that its members were fully aware of the complex forces that had brought the constitutional issue finally before them. As the Court set about formulating its decision it confronted a wide range of possible findings—a range limited only by the uncertain boundaries of the law and the ingenuity of its members. Between the extremes of maintaining *Plessy* without change, and a court order flatly declaring segregation in education unconstitutional, there appeared to be at least eight primary possibilities:

1. That there was no need to rule on the constitutionality of segregation *per se*, since each case might be disposed of on other grounds. (The Supreme Court had repeatedly declared that it would not rule on questions of a constitutional nature if a case could be decided by any other means.)

2. That the "separate but equal" doctrine was still the law, and when the separate facilities were unequal the Court would allow a reasonable period for the facilities to be made equal in fact.

3. That the "separate but equal" doctrine was still the law, but when separate facilities were unequal the Court would require immediate admission of Negroes to the white schools pending the achievement of actual equality of facilities.

4. That the "separate but equal" doctrine was still the law, but the Court might require non-segregation in certain phases of public education which it deemed impossible of equality within the separate framework. (In other words, the Court might conceivably hold that a particular course or activity could not be provided equally under segregation, as it had at least implied in the higher education cases.)

5. That whether segregation in a given case was a denial of equal protection of the laws was a question of fact, to be decided as are other questions of fact in the lower trial court.

6. That segregation was unconstitutional; the Court recognized the need for orderly progress of transition to non-segregation; but the Court would limit itself to minimum personal relief of the plaintiffs, leaving to Congress the job of legislating detailed rules for implementing de-segregation in the schools generally. (This would be in keeping with the idea that the administration of local school systems involves a "political question.")

7. That "separate but equal" was a clear denial of equal protection of the laws and thus unconstitutional; but the Court would permit a gradual change-over to a non-segregated system under the supervision of the District Courts, or under the direction of a master appointed by the Supreme Court itself.

8. That "separate but equal" was unconstitutional and must be ended immediately; Negro plaintiffs in the cases before the Court must be admitted at once to the white schools.

Whatever the Court's decision might be it was obvious that it would have a profound effect on public education in the United States. But that impact would center only upon the seventeen states where separate schools are prescribed by constitutional provision, by statute, or by both, and upon the District of Columbia. These are the Southern and border states—Alabama, Arkansas, Delaware, Florida, Georgia, Kentucky, Louisiana, Maryland, Mississippi, Missouri, North Carolina, Oklahoma, South Carolina, Tennessee, Texas, Virginia, and West Virginia. The four states which have permissive statutes have small Negro populations and no substantial changes would result.

CHAPTER ELEVEN

Closing the Gaps

THE SOUTH'S DEFENSE IN THE PUBLIC SCHOOL LITIGATION rested squarely on the *Plessy* doctrine, and in so casting it the region accepted the full burden of providing absolute equality in the educational facilities provided for the two races—at least within the limits of each applicable administrative unit. Implied, and sometimes openly stated, was a plea of guilty to omissions of the past; Governor Byrnes of South Carolina said candidly: "To meet this situation we are forced to do now what we should have been doing for the last fifty years."

As the Supreme Court undertook its deliberations the South could still hope that it would be allowed to provide equality in its own way, but it had to recognize that the time for temporizing was rapidly running out. And it also had to recognize that the old catch phrase "equalization" was a simple term with a complex meaning.

The courts, in their consideration of the specific cases before them, had provided a wide range of measurements that might be used to establish the size of the job ahead. There had been appraisals based on the size, arrangement and appearance of buildings; on the adequacy of physical equipment, toilets, basketball courts, drinking fountains, laboratory capacity, and textbooks; on the distance children must travel to school; and even on the condition of the roads over which they must pass. The courts had also taken into account the number of courses in the curriculum, the length of the school term, the professional qualifications of the teachers, and the pupil grading or promotion system. Extra-curricular activities, including athletic programs, had been weighed in the balance. On the college level weight had even been given to an institution's traditions or lack of them.

All of these factors, however, could be translated into fiscal terms—and always were by the courts. On the capital investment side it might be that the per pupil outlay for Negroes would have to be unduly heavy until parity was reached, but thereafter it could be assumed that an even-handed disbursement would keep the system in balance. And on the operating side, equalization of per pupil expenditure could be expected to bring about equalization of teacher salaries and overall programs.

At the beginning of 1954 all the Southern states had completed detailed studies of the discrepancies in their dual school systems or were in the process of making them. But schoolmen have had to recognize—as the public often has not—that the gap between white and Negro schools is only one aspect of the region's total educational problem, and that there is no way that it can be considered apart from the overall deficiencies of the Southern school system.

The general disparity between white and Negro schools has its counterpart in the inequalities between urban and rural schools in the South. In every state there are counties in which the best white school by any standard of comparison is inferior to the worst Negro schools in the larger cities. And the educational problems of the rural South have been increased by recent population trends, which in the decade after 1940 saw a net loss of 4.2 million people in the farm areas of the thirteen states.

Farm incomes have risen, but the thinning out of rural population has also tended to reduce the local resources upon which rural schools still depend in large part. And actual or potential reductions in rural pupil loads have been offset by more widely scattered school enrollment. This changing situation has been met by the movement toward consolidation of rural school facilities begun many years ago for whites and more recently for Negroes. Consolidation, however, has not been an economy move, but a practical effort to improve the educational facilities available to a dispersed population. The new central schools are providing facilities, services, courses of instruction, and extra-curricular programs that were not possible in the days of the one- or two-room country schoolhouse, but the per-pupil cost of operating these new consolidated facilities is considerably higher.

Recent improvements in the South's rural schools have only begun to scratch the surface of the accumulated deficiencies—even though the proportion of state funds channeled to them through equalization programs has risen sharply. In 1940 the breakdown of school revenue in eleven Southern states showed $129,053,000 from local sources and $131,897,000 in state and federal funds. In 1952 the same schools received $379,530,000 from local sources and $626,-489,000 from state and federal funds—the great bulk of it state money. But in the same period the gap between per pupil instruction expenditures in metropolitan and rural counties had widened from $20 to $44, and in capital outlay from approximately $2 to almost $37.

Quantitatively, the rural schools have made great progress since 1940. The percentage of children not attending school regularly is not now significantly larger than the percentage for metropolitan areas, and the length of school terms—which showed a considerable gap in 1940—is now about the same. The differential in teacher-pupil ratio is negligible.

The gap in per pupil expenditure between urban and rural schools now shows up primarily in qualitative differences, which are much more difficult to measure. (See Chart 7.) In the basic computation of years of college completed, rural teachers now have about one-half a year less training than those in urban communities, against a gap of about three-quarters of a year in 1940. But these figures do not reflect the fact that the rural schools have been providing a training ground for the city systems, with turnover in personnel running as high as 75 per cent a year in many rural systems. The city schools, with much higher salaries and more desirable living conditions, often fill their vacancies with the best qualified of the rural teachers with the result that many rural schools have experienced a steady decline in the standards of instruction in recent years.

The overall financial differential between the rural and urban systems, of course, reflects the fact that the disparities between white and Negro schools are much greater in rural areas than in the cities—where, in fact, the dollar gap has been closing rapidly. (See Chart 8.) The practical effect of this, however, is to place the greatest burden of Negro-white equalization upon districts which are least able to afford it, and which face the prospect of sacrificing their continuing effort to pull up the level of their sub-standard white schools. The state equalization programs have drawn their greatest political support from rural areas, and this was true even before the Negro-white equalization drive became a factor. Thus rural legislators, who carry disproportionate weight in most Southern legislatures, are often at odds with city representatives, whose constituents recognize that they will receive little immediate return from increased state school taxes even

7 THE URBAN-RURAL GAP IS CLOSING
CURRENT EXPENDITURES PER PUPIL

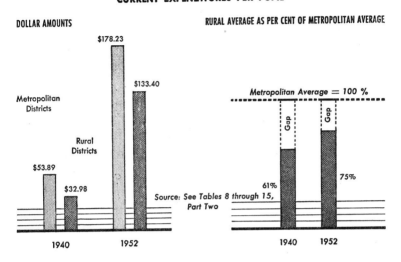

DOLLAR AMOUNTS

RURAL AVERAGE AS PER CENT OF METROPOLITAN AVERAGE

$178.23

$133.40

Metropolitan Districts

Metropolitan Average = 100 %

Rural Districts

Gap   Gap

$53.89

$32.98

75%

61%

Source: See Tables 8 through 15, Part Two

1940   1952

1940   1952

8 THE WHITE-NEGRO GAP IS GREATER IN RURAL AREAS
CURRENT EXPENDITURES PER PUPIL, 1952

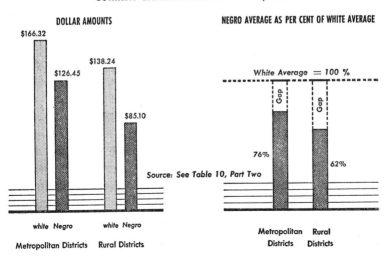

DOLLAR AMOUNTS

NEGRO AVERAGE AS PER CENT OF WHITE AVERAGE

$166.32

$126.45

$138.24

White Average = 100 %

$85.10

Gap   Gap

76%

62%

Source: See Table 10, Part Two

white Negro   white Negro

Metropolitan Districts   Rural Districts

Metropolitan   Rural
Districts   Districts

though they will bear the heaviest share of the burden. This basic political conflict is bound to color any effort toward educational equalization with its emphasis on Negro schools.

The decentralization which characterizes the administration of most Southern public school systems has sometimes made it difficult for state authorities to insure that funds allocated to local districts for Negro-white equalization will be spent for that purpose. Where white school systems are sub-standard, the temptation is great for local officials to divert to white use state money earmarked for Negro schools. For example, in March 1953 a special investigating committee of the Mississippi Legislature in a sharply critical report said: "In many counties money specifically appropriated for equalizing the pay of Negro teachers which was sent to the counties for that purpose never got to the Negro teachers."

These internal deficiencies of the Southern educational system, as measured in the gaps between facilities available to white and Negro and urban and rural children, contribute heavily to the disparity between the region's schools and those of the rest of the nation. Since the turn of the century Southerners have increasingly turned to education as the ultimate solvent for the region's economic and social problems. "Education governors," such as Charles B. Aycock in North Carolina, have come to power in most of the states at one time or another, preaching the gospel of universal schooling with evangelical fervor and basing their political programs primarily on the drive to better the public schools. For many years Southerners have demonstrated their faith by spending a higher proportion of their total personal income for education than has the rest of the nation; in the last year of record the proportion stood at 3.3 per cent for the South against 2.7 per cent for the non-South. (See Chart 9 and Table 1.)

9 INCOME AND SCHOOL EXPENDITURES, 1950

The Southern States have relatively low incomes, but most of them are spending a high proportion for public schools . . . . .

PER CAPITA INCOME	PUBLIC SCHOOL EXPENDITURES as a Per Cent of Total Personal Income
1. Delaware — $1956	1. Arizona — 4.5
2. Nevada — $1882	2. New Mexico — 4.3
3. New York — $1872	3. Louisiana — 4.0
4. Connecticut — $1789	4. Oregon — 4.0
5. Illinois — $1757	5. North Carolina — 3.9
6. California — $1750	6. Utah — 3.8
7. New Jersey — $1708	7. Oklahoma — 3.6
8. Washington — $1627	8. Idaho — 3.5
9. Massachusetts — $1602	9. Arkansas — 3.4
10. Michigan — $1596	10. South Carolina — 3.3
11. Ohio — $1584	11. Tennessee — 3.3
12. Montana — $1568	12. California — 3.3
13. Maryland — $1557	13. Montana — 3.3
14. Rhode Island — $1542	14. West Virginia — 3.3
15. Pennsylvania — $1537	15. Wyoming — 3.3
16. Oregon — $1517	16. Colorado — 3.2
17. Wyoming — $1514	17. North Dakota — 3.2
18. Nebraska — $1474	18. South Dakota — 3.2
19. Indiana — $1459	19. Alabama — 3.1
20. Wisconsin — $1442	20. Texas — 3.1
21. Iowa — $1413	21. Iowa — 3.1
22. Missouri — $1396	22. Minnesota — 3.0
23. Colorado — $1384	23. Washington — 2.9
24. Kansas — $1349	24. Florida — 2.8
25. Minnesota — $1343	25. Virginia — 2.8
26. New Hampshire — $1310	26. Kansas — 2.8
27. South Dakota — $1275	27. Mississippi — 2.7
28. North Dakota — $1273	28. Maryland — 2.7
29. Texas — $1273	29. Michigan — 2.7
30. Utah — $1270	30. Indiana — 2.7
31. Idaho — $1260	31. Georgia — 2.6
32. Arizona — $1233	32. Nevada — 2.6
33. Florida — $1201	33. Vermont — 2.6
34. Vermont — $1162	34. New Hampshire — 2.5
35. Maine — $1157	35. New Jersey — 2.5
36. Virginia — $1147	36. Kentucky — 2.4
37. New Mexico — $1133	37. Maine — 2.4
38. Oklahoma — $1077	38. Nebraska — 2.4
39. West Virginia — $1050	39. Wisconsin — 2.4
40. Louisiana — $1049	40. Connecticut — 2.3
41. Georgia — $967	41. Illinois — 2.3
42. Tennessee — $967	42. Ohio — 2.3
43. North Carolina — $949	43. New York — 2.2
44. Kentucky — $913	44. Pennsylvania — 2.2
45. Alabama — $847	45. Delaware — 2.1
46. South Carolina — $844	46. Missouri — 2.0
47. Arkansas — $821	47. Massachusetts — 1.9
48. Mississippi — $703	48. Rhode Island — 1.8

Source: See Table 1, Part Two

Although there is still a substantial dollar gap between school expenditures in the South and the non-South, the record of dollars spent is not an exact measurement of the comparative quality of the Southern and non-Southern school systems. Southern schools benefit from generally lower wage scales which are reflected in teachers' pay, and from lower building costs which are determined not only by the wage differential but by the fact that the milder climate permits lighter construction. The preponderance of rural schools also means a considerable overall saving in site costs. The fact remains, however, that by all the usual measurements Southern schools still lag below national standards, and Southern educators have long since dedicated themselves to closing that gap as well as all the others.

The legal drive for equalization of Negro facilities has already had a sharp impact upon the whole of the Southern educational structure—and in a purely economic sense that pressure will not be materially different whether the dual school system is maintained or reorganized in the direction of integration. Along with this has come the less dramatic but equally persistent pressure to close the gap between rural and urban schools for the children of both races. When the South counts up its school dollars these days it does so in the realization that it can no longer take up any part of the slack by depriving its Negro citizens of a proportionate share of school revenue—nor can it delay meeting the other commitments it long ago set for itself.

The size and the shape of the task ahead of the region in the next decade has been measured by a staff of educators and economists in a study undertaken for this report. Their findings, as presented here in severely digested form, are subject to obvious limitations. To begin with, summary figures for the South as a whole tend to smooth out the great variations from state to state and from school district to school district within each state. For example, the fact that in the South as a whole the operating deficit for Negro schools has been cut to 6 per cent of the total operating budget tends to obscure the equally relevant fact that there are still districts where local school taxes would have to be doubled if the racial discrepancy in per pupil expenditures were to be wiped out at a stroke. Moreover, because of the many variables which enter into the picture, it is impossible to prepare a region-wide measurement with pinpoint accuracy. Therefore, the analysis which follows does not pretend to be a prediction or a precise estimate. It is intended merely to give a rough approximation of the magnitude of the task which lies ahead of the South.

The several deficits that beset public education in the South must be measured in two ways—in terms of current expenditures for day-to-day operation of the schools, and in terms of capital expenditures for school buildings and equipment. The term "current expenditures" does not ordinarily include debt service and other indirect costs, but in the following analysis these items are included because they represent costs which must be paid from current school income.

The region's white-Negro gap in current expenditures is already closing at an accelerating rate. In some areas, particularly in the large cities, the deficit has been wiped out altogether, and even in the rural areas the disparity has been shrinking year by year. If every Southern community equalized per pupil current expenditures for Negroes and whites in the 1953-54 school year, the additional cost for the thirteen states would be about $90 million—or about 6 per cent of the region's current annual operating budget. If, in addition to closing the white-Negro gap, the South also undertook to close the urban-rural gap, it would require a further increase of about $240 million in current expenditures this year to bring the average rural per-pupil expenditure up to the average of the metropolitan areas, which is estimated at $200 per pupil. These two increases would add about 23 per cent to the region's estimated actual current expenditures of $1,450 million for the 1953-54 school year, and would raise the total to $1,780 million. (See Panel 1, Chart 10.)

A comparable measurement of the capital deficit, however, is considerably more complex. On the basis of "book value"—that is, original cost less depreciation—the per pupil worth of buildings and equipment in the South is about $190 less for Negroes than for whites, adding up to an aggregate deficit of about $350 million. Although it is impossible to translate this "book value" exactly into new building and equipment costs, this figure may be taken as a conservative estimate of the cost of equalizing the physical facilities now available to the two races.

In their own approach to measuring the physical deficiencies of their public school systems most state officials in the South—in recognition of a broader goal than mere racial "equalization," and of political reality—have incorporated the deficiencies of the Negro schools into the larger outline of overall "capital deficit programs." These are predicated upon the elimination of all sub-standard schools— white as well as Negro—and they provide a far more practical measure of the job ahead.

The total of these capital deficit programs, which are based on local cost estimates and building standards rather than the national averages employed by NEA and other agencies, currently stands at about $1.7 billion. (A measure of the South's recent progress may be seen in the fact that on the same basis the capital deficit was estimated in 1952 at $2.1 billion.) Of the $1.7 billion total, about $600 million would be needed for new Negro facilities, which would include the estimated $350 million required to "equalize" Negro schools with existing white facilities, many of which are also sub-standard. This means that about one-third of the current capital deficit is now accounted for by Negro facilities, although Negroes make up only about one-fourth of the total school population.

Besides the task of replacing sub-standard schools for both races, the South is also faced with the urgent need of providing additional classrooms to accommodate net additions to its school population. Present estimates indicate that by 1962 the South's average daily school attendance will reach about 9,100,000 pupils, an increase of about 16 per cent over the current school year. The region's building program is already subject to the special pressures created by the shift in population from rural to urban areas. This brings about a greater demand for new facilities than even the rapid increase in attendance would indicate, with new consolidated structures required in rural areas of declining population while new buildings must also be built in the growing metropolitan suburbs. It is estimated that the cost of new facilities—quite apart from the cost of eliminating the present capital deficit for both races—would be about $1.3 billion.

The $1.7 billion in capital outlays required to eliminate sub-standard white and Negro schools would be clearly beyond the South's financial capacity to handle in any one year. For purposes of this analysis, it is spread over eight years, as is the $1.3 billion for new facilities. This would mean an annual outlay of $375 million. (See Panel 2, Chart 10.)

White-Negro "equalization," then, considered in the perspective of the total needs of the South's school system, would become a secondary item in a budget that also took into account the increasing school population, urban-rural equalization, and a modest degree of general improvement. If the South undertook to meet all of these needs by 1962, its total

10· WHAT THE SOUTH WOULD HAVE TO SPEND

TODAY . . . . . IN CURRENT EXPENDITURES ➡

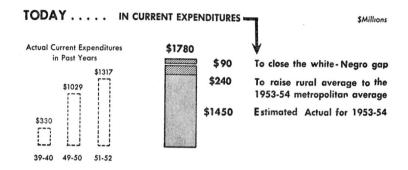

$Millions

Actual Current Expenditures in Past Years

$330 — 39-40
$1029 — 49-50
$1317 — 51-52

$1780

$90   To close the white-Negro gap

$240   To raise rural average to the 1953-54 metropolitan average

$1450   Estimated Actual for 1953-54

OVER THE NEXT 8 YEARS . . . . . FOR NEW CLASSROOMS ➡

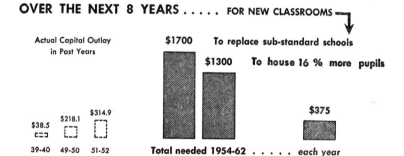

Actual Capital Outlay in Past Years

$38.5 — 39-40
$218.1 — 49-50
$314.9 — 51-52

$1700   To replace sub-standard schools

$1300   To house 16 % more pupils

$375

Total needed 1954-62 . . . . . each year

IN 1962 . . . . . TO ACHIEVE THESE GAINS ➡

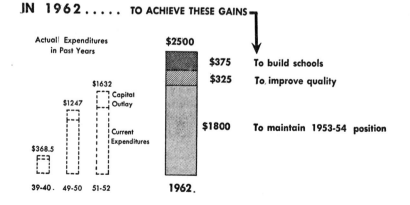

Actual Expenditures in Past Years

$368.5 — 39-40
$1247 — 49-50
$1632 — 51-52

Capital Outlay
Current Expenditures

$2500

$375   To build schools

$325   To improve quality

$1800   To maintain 1953-54 position

1962

11 THE SOUTH COULD ACHIEVE THESE GAINS BY 1962

If its income keeps rising . . . . .   *and it continues to spend 3.3 per cent of its income on schools . . . . .*

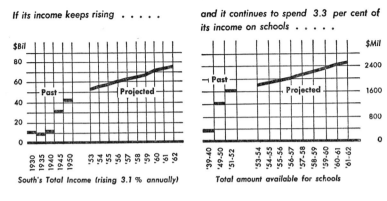

South's Total Income (rising 3.1 % annually)   Total amount available for schools

BUT A HUGE TASK OF RAISING QUALITY WOULD REMAIN

As suggested by these comparisons in current expenditures per pupil . . . . .

Southern Regional Average

If the gains are achieved **1962**

Actual in   **1952**

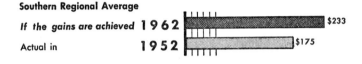

Metropolitan Averages in Selected Southern States

Kentucky
Louisiana
Oklahoma   **1952**
Texas
Florida
Virginia

Selected State Averages Elsewhere in the U. S.

Delaware
Oregon
Wyoming
Nevada
Arizona   **1951**
Wisconsin
Minnesota
New Mexico
New Hampshire

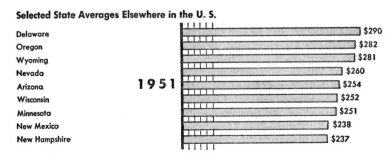

school bill in that year would amount to about $2.5 billion, an increase of more than 50 per cent over the 1951-52 figure. About $1.8 billion in current expenditures would be required to accommodate an average daily attendance of 9,100,000 and to maintain white-Negro equalization. To raise operating expenditures in rural schools to the 1953-54 level of metropolitan schools and to allow for a very modest improvement ($37 million) in city schools would cost an additional $325 million in operating expenditures. And finally, to meet the last annual payment on the capital program would cost $375 million. (See Panel 3, Chart 10.)

Could the South afford these costs? The answer is yes—if its income continues to rise at the rate of 3.1 per cent a year, and if it continues to spend 3.3 per cent of its income on public schools. (See Panels 1 and 2, Chart 11.) But even if all of these gains were achieved, a huge task would remain. White and Negro current expenditures per pupil would be equalized in each community, substandard schools for both races would be eliminated, additional schools would be provided to meet the increase in attendance, current expenditures in rural schools would be brought up to the 1953-54 level of metropolitan schools, and there would be a slight improvement in city schools. But the estimates for 1962 stop there. They make no allowance for the cost of the additional improvement in the quality of Southern education which would be necessary to lift the standards of the entire system. The best schools in the larger cities of the South are probably as good as any in the nation, yet thoughtful Southerners, like their contemporaries everywhere, doubt that even these are good enough. So there are continuing campaigns to raise teachers' salaries, expand and revise programs of instruction, and in other ways move toward the optimum levels advocated by professional educators. It is impossible to estimate the exact effect these pressures will have on expenditures for what might be called the standard-setting schools of the South over the next decade. But the magnitude of the task that would remain even after the gaps were closed is indicated by the fact that in 1962, under the projected estimates, the South's average current expenditures per pupil (including debt service and other indirect costs) would still be lower than the comparable 1952 average of metropolitan counties in two Southern states, and well below the 1951 average of many states outside the South. (See Panel 3, Chart 11.)

The foregoing analysis is of course a rough sketch of the task ahead and not a blueprint. For example, there is no guarantee that the South will continue to bring industry and agriculture into balance, and improve its per capita income, at the present rate. A general contraction of the national economy is already being felt in the region—and if it continues it conceivably could have a disproportionate impact as it did in the thirties. It is by no means certain that the South will continue to tax itself at the present high rate for education. And finally, there is no reason to believe that the region will approach these problems with any degree of consistency: greater emphasis may be placed on one facet of the educational problem in one state than another; some states almost certainly will move generally ahead at a more rapid rate than others; and the vagaries of politics may well plunge some states into an educational "recession."

It is possible that intensified legal pressures in the wake of the Supreme Court decision might lead some states to the conscious decision to freeze white schools at present levels while concentrating all additional funds upon improvement of Negro facilities—although this seems to be politically unlikely. A sharp increase in state and local school taxes would have the same effect; stepping up the percentage of the South's income devoted to the schools, for example, would make it possible to complete the total equalization process in a shorter time span. Actually, however, the tendency seems to be the other way, for school appropriations in the South now have to compete with pressing demands for other services and facilities as the process of industrialization continues, with most communities in the "investment stage" which calls for heavy outlays before compensating higher tax returns are realized.

A far more tangible possibility of speeding the closing of the gap is federal aid to education. Measures providing for federal appropriations to insure nationwide equalization of educational opportunity are hardy perennials in Congress, and they have the potent backing of state and national education associations. The South would be an obvious beneficiary of any such program, but fear of its possible impact upon the bi-racial system has led many Southern congressmen to oppose it in the past. Some have gone along when clear safeguards for local determination of policy were written into the bills, but others have argued that such legislation is always subject to change—and that the threat of stringent anti-segregation provisions, which have always been advocated by the NAACP and many non-Southern legislators, is inherent in federal aid. Even so, the South has provided effective leadership in the drive for a federal school program. Senator Richard Russell of Georgia, who is generally identified as leader of the conservative Democrats, has been a proponent, and Senator Lister Hill of Alabama led a faction that sought to head off the transfer of oil-bearing tidelands to the states with a bill that would have earmarked the proceeds of these oil reserves for the public schools. Early in 1954 Senator John L. McClellan of Arkansas announced that he would sponsor legislation providing for matching federal funds for school construction, to be distributed on a basis of need which would favor the Southern states. In his 1954

State of the Union message President Eisenhower endorsed the principle of federal aid for school construction.

No weight has been given in these economic projections to the possibility of integration of the dual school system because, contrary to popular argument, segregation has not been an important separate factor in school costs until now and is not likely to be in the immediate future.

The South is only now reaching the point where there are enough classrooms and enough teachers to meet the minimum demand of its children for education. There has been general discrimination against Negroes, it is true, but it could have been corrected only by pouring additional money into the total system or by lowering the standards of white schools. If at any point in the past discrimination had been wiped out by total integration the effect would have been that some Negroes would have gone to better schools and some whites to worse—but no appreciable economies would have resulted to make additional funds available for improvement of the total system.

It is true that examples of waste can be cited. Some rural counties with sparse Negro population have paid high transportation costs to haul Negroes long distances to a segregated school in a neighboring district rather than admit them to a local white school. And there are occasional cases where an underpopulated Negro school might be eliminated entirely if Negro pupils were permitted to attend a nearby underpopulated white school. There are still other types of situations in which communities are paying a substantial price for maintaining segregated schools. But in the aggregate these cases do not yet add up to anything approaching a determinant in school finance in the region.

The same basic factors hold true in projections for the decade ahead. If Negroes and whites were immediately reshuffled through the whole of the school system, the same general deficiencies in physical facilities, teacher training, curricula, and the like would exist. Abstract justice might be achieved, in that the deficit would then fall evenly upon members of both races, but the overall standards of public education would not be materially improved.

As the South continues to build its total school system, however, and as emphasis is placed upon qualitative rather than quantitative improvement, these factors will change. The continuing migration from rural to urban areas, with its resultant reduction in the proportion of Negroes to whites in many rural counties, will likewise tend to make the maintenance of separate but equal schools increasingly expensive in many districts, and shifting population patterns in the cities will produce the same result in "fringe" areas where white and Negro communities overlap. Thus a real economic pressure toward integration will build up. Many Southern school officials have recognized this in their long-range projections and have quietly opposed as unrealistic the wholesale appropriation of funds to build new Negro schools as a safeguard against possible court action. The shift in the population base is so rapid that schools built to serve present concentrations of Negroes might be wholly or partially empty within a decade.

There has been little public discussion of integration of the public schools in the South and no official planning to accomplish it—for the good reason that public policy, still firmly buttressed by dominant public attitudes, is opposed to it. Yet many schoolmen, and many politicians for that matter, privately concede that integration is coming—not overnight and not necessarily as a direct result of the present school litigation, but as a result of the larger trends of which it is a symptom. In the long run the big questions are when? and how?

CHAPTER TWELVE

The South and the Issue

THE SOUTH OF SONG AND STORY HAS ALWAYS BEEN A MISLEAD-
ing stereotype, yet it intrudes upon any discussion of the
region and its peculiar institutions—as it did in the arguments on educational segregation presented to the Supreme
Court. In neither a geographic nor a cultural sense are the
seventeen states which now require segregation in the public
schools a true commonalty. The primary considerations
that bind them together in this instance are the proportion
of their Negro population (which is significantly diminish-
ing) and the legal devices by which they have sought to
maintain separation of the races (in which there is a wide
variety). The demographers identify four sub-regions, and
even the students of linguistics have discovered two Souths,
in many ways as markedly different in background and outlook as they are in accent.

The Lowland South—principally the Atlantic and Gulf
coastal plains, the sand hill areas, and the delta country of
the Mississippi Valley—includes what is often called the
Black Belt, in reference to its soil as well as its population.
This is the area where great plantations once flourished, and
sometimes still do, and where the vestiges of a feudal society
are still plainly visible. Here is the greatest concentration

of Southern Negroes; here are the counties where Negro population often exceeds the white, and where the legal requirements of segregation are secondary to the powerful social and economic forces that buttress rigid separation of the races.

In the Upland South—the mountainous areas and the smaller strip of Piedmont country which contains most of the region's industrial centers—Negroes have always been fewer and local traditions have different roots. There were occasional plantations here too, but they were the exception to the prevailing pattern of family-worked farms. This is the historic domain of the Scotch-Irish, who have tended to be conservative in matters of social custom and liberal in politics.

Thus the impact of the legal forces working against racial segregation in the public schools has not fallen evenly upon the whole of the Southern region, any more than have the other legal and extra-legal forces which have re-defined the Southern Negro's status in little more than a generation. There are counties in the South which have no Negro population, and others where Negroes have become so few that segregation in the schools is already coming to be looked upon as a nuisance hardly worth bothering with. But there are also Southern counties where the sudden lowering of the color bar would mean that white children would find themselves in a considerable minority in a mixed public school system. In between lie the majority of the Southern school districts. (See Tables 23 and 24.)

The ratio of Negro to white population is not a final determinant of racial attitudes, but it is perhaps the most powerful single influence, for the practical results of desegregation depend heavily upon it. This, more than anything else, seems to account for the great variation in the degree of expressed concern in the South over the steadily rising status of the Negro in the last generation—which has led finally to the demand for admission to the white schools. The Upland South, for example, found little to alarm it in the Negro's successful legal battle for the ballot, for there his numbers are not sufficient to give him control of local politics. The whites in the Black Belt, however, have had to face the prospect of becoming members of a political minority and many of them are still resisting, although the only means left to them are extra-legal.

Certainly no white Southerner can ignore the abundant evidence that the walls of racial segregation are crumbling under persistent internal and external pressures. Yet the dominant white Southern attitude toward the process remains negative; if there are variations from state to state and from section to section, they are for the most part variations only in degree of adverse reaction—ranging from resigned acceptance to outraged protest.

President Truman's civil rights program in the late forties provided a significant test of Southern sentiment. The South split wide open when the Democratic convention of 1948 endorsed the presidential commission's proposals for federal fair employment practices legislation, an anti-lynching law, and a federal statute outlawing segregation on intra-state transportation. Not all the Southern Democrats abandoned the party, it is true, but no one of them supported the civil rights program when it came before Congress, and some who would be counted among the most faithful in all other matters joined in the protesting filibusters in the Senate.

It can be argued that political estimates of public sentiment are not infallible. But in this instance the instinctive reaction of the politicians has the support of the South's ranking sociologist. In the forties Professor Howard W. Odum of the University of North Carolina in *Race and*

Rumors of Race attempted to distill a composite Southern credo from what he has called "a sort of hidden poll of the great mass of Southern folk." At its heart he identified a central theme: "The Negro is a Negro, and nothing more." It was difficult, he said, for many Southern leaders to accept the fact that this baldly-stated concept remained the essence of Southern folkways after all the years that had passed since emancipation. Yet Odum concluded: "It was of the utmost importance that Southerners face the plain assumption that they did not appraise the Negro as the same sort of human being as they themselves are."

How long this credo will survive the swift flow of contemporary events is, of course, a matter of conjecture. The most significant of the changes in the traditional pattern—the emergence of the Negro as a voting citizen of the South—is too recent to have produced profound positive results, but certainly the negative influence of his ballot is being felt within the general framework of a segregated society. Politicians have already discovered that the enfranchised Negro cannot be safely ignored, or treated as a ward of charity, in the distribution of public funds. Moreover, he has begun to attain increasing immunity from the direct political attacks with which he became painfully familiar in the days before he had the vote. Some white Southern politicians are now openly seeking Negro support, and most of the others are becoming increasingly cautious about alienating the mass of Negro voters. In every Southern state there is now the mathematical possibility that Negroes, voting as a bloc, could swing the balance of power.

The South fought on every legal front to preserve the white primary—which was the historic device for disfranchising the Negro—just as it is now battling to maintain segregated public schools. When the courts ruled that the primaries were an integral part of the electoral process and therefore subject to the guaranties of the federal constitution, South Carolina—which now threatens to abandon the public school system if segregation is outlawed—went to the extreme of repealing its state election laws and re-constituting the state Democratic party as a private organization. Yet when the courts ruled that last resort out of bounds Negroes began to go to the polls in South Carolina without provoking the widespread violence that had been so freely prophesied. Neither, it should be noted, has their exercise of the franchise yet brought about any significant change in the pattern of South Carolina politics.

In one important respect, however, the enfranchisement of the Negro does not provide an exact analogy to the ending of segregation in the public schools. The presence of the Negro in the voting place heretofore reserved for whites does not necessarily connote what white Southerners call "social equality"; on the other hand mixed schools involve a sustained personal contact between the races that touches upon the peculiarly sensitive area of Southern family life. In the drive to end lynching, to wipe out racial discrimination before the courts, to obtain equal school facilities, and even to obtain the ballot the Negro has had substantial and effective support from white Southerners, who could and usually did argue that no real question of social equality was involved in any of this. In his demand for an end to segregation in the public schools, however, the Negro has stood almost alone.

Indeed, it is a standard argument that the rank and file of Southern Negroes do not support the effort—that it stems entirely from the militant Negro leadership which now centers in the NAACP. Governor Byrnes of South Carolina, who served as a sort of *ex officio* spokesman for his gubernatorial colleagues in the period of the Supreme Court test, said: "Except for the professional agitators, what the colored people want, and what they are entitled to, is equal facilities in their schools." The point is hotly disputed by Negro spokesmen inside and outside the South, and it is not likely to be settled soon since the great mass of Southern Negroes is still inarticulate in all public matters. Nothing comparable to Professor Odum's analysis of white Southern attitudes has ever been attempted for the minority race. There can be no doubt, however, that the new Negro leadership—still heavily reliant upon intellectuals for the most part—is determined that segregation must go in every phase of American life. A measure of this may be seen in the fact that a symposium of leading Negro educators held at Howard University two decades ago was devoted entirely to discussion of ways and means of improving the Negro schools under the *Plessy* "separate but equal" doctrine. A similar gathering at Howard in 1952 was aptly described by its official title: "The Courts and Racial Integration in Education." Whether the mass of Southern Negroes shares the almost religious dedication of their leaders is debatable; there is no reason to doubt their emotional orientation toward the goal of full equality, but the scant record to date would seem to indicate a greater tendency toward compromise among the rank and file. Perhaps the most significant development in this regard is that there *is* an active and vocal indigenous Negro leadership—where a generation ago the Southern Negro depended primarily upon sympathetic Southern whites to present his cause before the public.

The debate over segregation, in the schools or anywhere else, touches deep emotions. Advocates on both sides tend to argue their case in terms of principle rather than practice; the legal action before the Supreme Court was often treated as though it were Armageddon, when in long perspective it may turn out to be no more than one more milestone in the long road the Negro has traveled since he was brought to this continent in chains. At the time when the Georgia legislature was attempting to work out ways and means of divorcing the public school system from state control as a safeguard against a possible Court decision against segregation, Ralph McGill, the editor of the influential *Atlanta Constitution,* wrote:

What the various state legislatures are doing, as they busy themselves with plans to carry on school segregation without legal compulsion, is admitting segregation by law is finished . . . either this year, next or within the next few to come. . . .

As a matter of fact, segregation has been on its way out for a good long time and has been breaking down at the edges for more than a generation. . . . Two great forces have been at work on segregation and the problem of race. One is secular, the other religious. The Christian of today cannot help but wince at the full implications, and the jarring clash of his creed, with discrimination against any person because of color. . . . Christianity cannot well afford to be on the wrong side of a moral force, as it was in some areas when it defended slavery.

The other influence is secular. Segregation implies inferiority. There are those who argue that it does not. But those segregated believe it does. . . . Across two great wars now we, along with other free peoples, have preached the rights of men everywhere to be free and equal—we have encouraged long-oppressed peoples to rise. . . .

An end to segregation—when it comes—will not, of course, force people to associate socially. That will remain, as now, personal choice. But it will bring on change—and this is what state legislatures in South Carolina, Georgia, Mississippi, Virginia and Alabama are, or will be, considering. They consider not how to retain legal segregation—which they see soon ending—but how to effect it without legal compulsion. . . . Segregation is on the way out and he who tries to tell the people otherwise does them great disservice. The problem of the future is how to live with the change.

The distinction made here between *legal* and *de facto* segregation is essential to any consideration of the future of bi-racial education in the United States. The limit of Supreme Court action is the setting of a new legal precedent; even if segregation in the public schools were flatly declared unconstitutional, integration would be ordered only in the five school districts cited in the five specific cases. No change would necessarily occur in the other 11,173 districts where segregation has been legal and usually practiced until and unless individual suits were brought against each administrative unit. This in itself guarantees a rather lengthy transition period. As long ago as 1938 the Court began enunciating the new points of law which led to the admission of Negroes to the graduate schools of Southern universities, yet fifteen years later the admission standards of five state universities in the South still remain inviolate and the number of Negro students on the de-segregated campuses still may be counted in the hundreds.

The great social and economic forces that have worked on behalf of segregation will keep on working regardless of judicial determination—just as will the forces working *against* segregation. Those on one side or the other have been bolstered by Court rulings in the past, but none has been wholly nullified.

The pattern of residential segregation which has sustained substantially segregated public schools in the cities of the non-South without the sanction of law is even more strictly observed in the urban South. The present school districts in most Southern cities, although there has never been any need for gerrymandering to insure separation of the races, would nevertheless produce the same general result.

In the rural areas, of course, segregation by calculated districting is not possible. There, however, the demand of Negroes for admission to white schools has always been weakest and the pressures against it strongest. It has been seen that the system of "voluntary" segregation is still common in the non-South; there is no reason to believe that a policy of free choice between all-white and all-Negro schools would not produce the same result in most Southern school districts, where the Negro community would be under even stronger public pressure to maintain the status quo.

Finally, there is the hard fact that integration in a meaningful sense cannot be achieved by the mere physical presence of children of two races in a single classroom. No public school is isolated from the community that supports it, and if the very composition of its classes is subject to deep-seated and sustained public disapproval it is hardly likely to foster the spirit of united effort essential to learning. Even those who are dedicated to the proposition that the common good demands the end of segregation in education cannot be unaware that if the transition produces martyrs they will be the young children who must bear the brunt of spiritual conflict.

This does not mean that the breaking down of legal segregation in the Southern schools would not have profound results. As McGill noted, it would mean change—not the revolution that both its proponents and its opponents have predicted, but an acceleration of processes already at work. Some school districts, which have been struggling with the economic problem of providing separate education for a handful of Negro children, would doubtless promptly drop their segregated schools. And as the present population trend continues to pull down the proportion of Negro population in the South, particularly in the rural areas, there will be more and more of these.

In any event the South has reached a point in its development where educators and laymen alike are going to have to take a close, new look at their educational problems. The unrealized goal of providing equal educational opportunity for all Southern children regardless of race—whether it be pursued under the separate-but-equal doctrine or through a process of gradual integration—demands that the Negro become an active partner, rather than a passive participant, in the formulation of educational policy. Already some Southern cities have seen Negroes elected to their local school boards with substantial white support or appointed by municipal authorities. Among them are Raleigh, Roanoke, Nashville, Newport News, Lynchburg, Richmond, Augusta, Atlanta, Knoxville, and Winston-Salem. Where school boards are elective and as yet have no Negro members, it has become a common practice to appoint Negro advisory groups to work with school officials.

This process, tentative though it still is, is of great significance. The fact is that the two races in the South have been growing apart for a generation; although still living side by side Negroes and whites have had less real communication in the past twenty-five years than ever before in the region's history. Their relationship in earlier days was basically that of master and servant, but it was nevertheless intimate and as it existed between individuals it was often based upon confidence and trust. The rising status of the Negro has now replaced the domestic who "lives on the place" with a part-time transient servant paid by the hour; the sawmill hand who once negotiated with his boss on the basis of their mutual memories of the boss's father is now represented by a union business agent; the tenant farmer with his personal identification with the land and its owners is rapidly being replaced by the day laborer. These are the hallmarks of economic and social progress for the Negro, but they also mark a process which has eroded away an historic interracial working relationship without effectively replacing it.

The transition from the tradition of *noblesse oblige,* which the Negro now rejects because of its connotations of inferiority, to a new concept of race relations is only beginning. The Negro's exercise of the legal weapons available to him under the *Plessy* doctrine provided a significant start, for here he did not appear as a supplicant but arose to demand equality of educational opportunity as his right. In many of these cases the state and federal district courts did not retreat to dry legalisms in reaching their decisions, but resorted to special techniques to work out what they could recognize were complex social problems. The court-sponsored conference between the Negro plaintiffs and their spokesmen and the white defendants and theirs became common—often with a specially-qualified arbiter sitting in at the court's invitation. Many of these decisions, certainly, were not based upon the letter of the law but upon a mutually acceptable accommodation worked out in free give and take across the table.

In many ways this is the end product of a process that began many years ago, and began, as such things must, at the very top of the educational structure. But where a half century ago Booker T. Washington and a handful of white Southern college presidents represented the outside limits of free and frank discussion of the mutual problems inherent in educating the two races, the level of discussion has now descended to the cross-roads hamlet and the participants are not learned educators but the parents of Negro children and the white laymen who sit on a local school board.

It is here that the South will have to determine the future of its educational system. Wise leadership at the upper levels can help, and emotional excursions by the leaders of either race can do great harm. But in the end the new patterns will have to be hammered out across the table in thousands of scattered school districts, and they will have to be shaped to accommodate not only the needs but the prejudices of whites and Negroes to whom these problems are not abstractions but the essence of their daily lives.

This process will place a special burden upon professional educators in the years ahead. In many cases they will find themselves cast in the role of "social engineers"—for the success or failure of their schools may come to depend not so much upon appropriations and physical facilities and curricula as upon the complex human relationships that divide or unite their communities.

As the South moves hesitantly into this new era there is no affirmative evidence to impeach the Southern credo defined by Professor Odum a decade ago, but there is abundant evidence that the South that produced it is undergoing a massive change. The economic time lag which kept the region at the rear of the great American industrial march is being wiped out, and the concepts of an industrial society are now contesting with those of the agrarians. The one-party South, which was itself the product of the effort to disfranchise the Negro, began its final dissolution in the last national election, when the region divided its votes between two candidates for president—this time for more complex reasons than the simple religious prejudice which split the Solid South in 1928. The South is still sending its sons out to seek opportunity in other regions, but it is now receiving in their stead a substantial number of managerial migrants come to operate its new factories and bringing with them national social and political concepts. All in all, the cultural, political, and economic isolation which is necessary to the preservation of the region's special identity is breaking down—and Southerners themselves are speeding the process in many ways, whether or not they are always pleased with the results.

In the long sweep of history the public school cases before the Supreme Court may be written down as the point at which the South cleared the last turning in the road to re-union—the point at which finally, and under protest, the region gave up its peculiar institutions and accepted the prevailing standards of the nation at large as the legal basis for its relationship with its minority race. This would not in itself bring about any great shift in Southern attitudes, nor even any far-reaching immediate changes in the pattern of bi-racial education. But it would re-define the goal the Southern people, white and Negro, are committed to seek in the way of democracy.

PART TWO

The Figures Tell the Story

The Figures Tell the Story

Part One of this book described the tremendous educational effort the South has made in recent years, the progress it has made toward closing the gaps between white-Negro and urban-rural education, the magnitude of the gaps that still remain, and the significance of the large-scale population shifts which have occurred during the past decade.

This part of the book illustrates these trends and developments through a series of tables prepared by the research team which did the spade work for this report.

The tables tell a fascinating story, underscoring many of the main points made in the first part of the book, giving new insights into the South's educational progress and problems, and doing a job which would have taken hundreds of pages of narrative to do—giving a state-by-state picture of the important changes which have been going on within the South in recent years.

I. SCHOOLS

THE SOUTH, ALTHOUGH HANDICAPPED BY A RELATIVELY LOWER income and a relatively higher educational load than the rest of the United States, has been making significant progress in public education in recent years. The rate of progress has varied from state to state, and from county to county within each state, but the overall trend has been upward. The gaps between white-Negro and urban-rural education have been closing, and the South as a whole has been drawing closer to the educational standards of the rest of the nation. However, the gaps between white-Negro and urban-rural education in the South are still substantial, particularly in terms of the relative adequacy of school facilities and the relative quality of educational offerings.

The progress which the South has been making, and the dimensions of the job that still lies ahead, are illustrated by Tables 1 through 15.

The data in the school tables are subject to two important limitations: (1) For the most part, they were compiled from records and reports of state departments of education, and the states do not keep records in a uniform manner; (2) The latest figures are for the school year 1951-52, so the tables do not reflect the further educational progress which the South has made in the past two years.

1. *Financial Ability and Educational Effort*

Although the South ranks far below the other regions of the United States in terms of per capita income, it ranks well above most of the rest of the nation in terms of the proportion of its income it has been spending for the education of its children in public schools.

As the following table indicates, the two states with the lowest per capita incomes in 1950—Mississippi and Arkansas—spent a larger proportion of their incomes on public schools than the two states with the highest per capita incomes—Delaware and New York. Louisiana, which ranked 41st in per capita income, ranked third in per cent of income spent on public schools.

The amount spent on schools in 1950 (Col. 3 of the table) includes total current expenditures, capital outlay, and interest in the school year 1949-50, rounded to the nearest tenth of a million dollars. It covers expenditures for day schools only, and does not include expenditures for summer, evening, and adult schools.

State	Per Capita Income 1950 (dollars)	Total Income 1950 (millions of dollars)	Amount Spent on Schools, 1950 (millions of dollars)	Per Cent of Income Spent on Schools
Alabama	$ 847	$2,581	$ 79.0	3.1%
Arizona	1,233	931	41.5	4.5
Arkansas	821	1,578	54.4	3.4
California	1,750	18,621	623.4	3.3
Colorado	1,384	1,840	59.5	3.2
Connecticut	1,789	3,598	83.4	2.3
Delaware	1,956	628	13.1	2.1
Florida	1,201	3,387	95.0	2.8
Georgia	967	3,336	88.9	2.6
Idaho	1,260	742	26.3	3.5
Illinois	1,757	15,400	358.2	2.3
Indiana	1,459	5,780	158.2	2.7
Iowa	1,413	3,725	114.2	3.1
Kansas	1,349	2,577	72.4	2.8
Kentucky	913	2,688	64.5	2.4
Louisiana	1,049	2,848	112.8	4.0
Maine	1,157	1,067	25.1	2.4
Maryland	1,557	3,420	93.2	2.7
Massachusetts	1,602	7,535	144.8	1.9
Michigan	1,596	10,242	274.5	2.7
Minnesota	1,343	3,995	118.2	3.0
Mississippi	703	1,527	40.8	2.7

Missouri	$1,396	$ 5,570	$112.5	2.0%
Montana	1,568	928	30.8	3.3
Nebraska	1,474	1,964	47.2	2.4
Nevada	1,882	303	8.8	2.6
New Hampshire	1,310	682	16.8	2.5
New Jersey	1,708	7,777	198.0	2.5
New Mexico	1,133	775	33.5	4.3
New York	1,872	28,381	610.7	2.2
North Carolina	*949*	*3,859*	*151.3*	*3.9*
North Dakota	1,273	788	24.9	3.2
Ohio	1,584	12,620	291.1	2.3
Oklahoma	*1,077*	*2,406*	*87.6*	*3.6*
Oregon	1,517	2,321	93.3	4.0
Pennsylvania	1,537	16,184	348.1	2.2
Rhode Island	1,542	1,217	21.5	1.8
South Carolina	*844*	*1,763*	*59.0*	*3.3*
South Dakota	1,275	835	27.1	3.2
Tennessee	*967*	*3,203*	*104.4*	*3.3*
Texas	*1,273*	*9,853*	*303.0*	*3.1*
Utah	1,270	880	33.6	3.8
Vermont	1,162	438	11.5	2.6
Virginia	*1,147*	*3,551*	*100.2*	*2.8*
Washington	1,627	3,875	112.8	2.9
West Virginia	1,050	2,115	69.7	3.3
Wisconsin	1,442	4,962	121.5	2.4
Wyoming	1,514	439	14.7	3.3

SOURCES: Data on income from *Survey of Current Business,* U.S. Department of Commerce, August, 1953. Data on school expenditures from "Statistics of State School Systems," *Biennial Survey of Education,* U.S. Office of Education, 1948-50, Col. 5, Table 30, P. 86.

2. *School Attendance in the South*

Between 1940 and 1950 average daily attendance in the South's public schools increased by 218,000, while in the rest of the United States taken as a whole there was almost no net gain. In the South, and probably also in the non-South, the two-year increase between 1950 and 1952 was greater than in the previous ten years. Although four Southern states showed losses in attendance between 1950 and 1952, there was an overall gain of 241,930 for the region as a whole.

In this and subsequent tables, the school years 1939-40, 1949-50, and 1951-52 are listed as calendar years 1940, 1950, and 1952, respectively. The attendance figures are for "average daily attendance," which is an accepted measure of attendance in the public schools. It is defined as the average number of children attending school on any given day. This, of course, is less than the number of children enrolled.

The term "public schools" in this and subsequent tables includes all elementary and secondary grades (kindergarten through the twelfth grade). The 1952 figure for North Carolina is for the school year 1950-51.

	1940	1950	1952	1950-52 Change
The U.S.	22,042,000	22,284,000		
U.S. outside the South	15,019,900	15,042,300		
South	7,022,133	7,240,521	7,482,451	241,930
Alabama	566,673	594,632	587,395	— 7,237
Arkansas	373,356	355,031	350,852	— 4,179
Florida	325,991	412,778	456,843	44,065
Georgia	583,875	619,846	637,529	17,683
Kentucky	493,210	480,256	477,605	— 2,651
Louisiana	398,114	420,740	445,710	24,970
Mississippi	474,020	472,149	471,469	— 680
N. Carolina	790,003	797,691	816,036	18,345
Oklahoma	484,896	401,931	404,767	2,836
S. Carolina	384,995	413,551	427,326	13,775
Tennessee	536,715	583,126	594,520	11,394
Texas	1,116,263	1,151,959	1,255,597	103,638
Virginia	494,022	536,831	556,802	19,971

SOURCES: State figures were compiled from data gathered by staff of the Southern States Cooperative Program in Educational Administration, from records and reports of state departments of education. U.S. and non-South figures are from "Statistics of State School Systems," *Biennial Survey of Education,* U.S. Office of Education.

3. *White and Negro School Children*

As measured by average daily atttendance, Negro children accounted for one-fourth of the South's public school population in 1952, but the proportion varied greatly among the states. Only one in sixteen of Kentucky's school children was Negro, while Negroes made up nearly half of the Mississippi total. White attendance increased more than Negro in the region as a whole between 1940 and 1952 but in five of the thirteen states, Negro attendance either gained more or declined less than white. The 1952 data for North Carolina are for the school year 1950-51.

	School Children in 1952			Per Cent Change since 1940	
	White	Negro	Per Cent Negro	White	Negro
South	5,580,450	1,902,001	25.4%	6.9%	5.7%
Alabama	383,679	203,716	34.7	3.7	3.6
Arkansas	268,235	82,617	23.5	— 5.6	— 7.2
Florida	344,319	112,524	24.6	44.1	29.3
Georgia	429,951	207,578	32.2	12.8	2.5
Kentucky	446,909	30,696	6.4	— 2.4	—13.3
Louisiana	276,662	169,048	37.9	9.0	17.1
Mississippi	244,605	226,864	48.1	— 1.1	.0
N. Carolina	576,117	239,919	29.4	2.9	4.2
Oklahoma	373,083	31,684	7.8	—16.6	—15.4
S. Carolina	244,889	182,437	42.7	9.9	12.5
Tennessee	496,574	97,946	16.5	11.1	8.9
Texas	1,079,063	176,534	14.1	14.4	2.1
Virginia	416,364	140,438	25.2	13.1	11.7

SOURCE: Compiled from data gathered by SSCPEA staff from records and reports of state departments of education.

4. *White Population and School Attendance*

Although the total white population of the South increased 16.5 per cent between 1940 and 1950, white school attendance increased only 3.1 per cent. The high postwar birth rate was just beginning to be reflected in attendance increases in the lower grades by 1950. Moreover, there were declines in the number of children in the upper grades due to the low birth rate of the thirties. The "big push" in school attendance was yet to come.

| | Per Cent Changes between 1940 and 1950 | | | |
| | Total White Population | White Population by Age Groups | | White School Attendance |
		5-9	10-14	15-17	
South	16.5%				3.1%
Alabama	12.5	11.2	— 6.2	— .2	4.8
Arkansas	1.1	2.5	—12.3	— .6	— 4.5
Florida	56.7	67.9	19.1	.2	28.7
Georgia	16.8	17.9	— 2.5	—1.4	8.4
Kentucky	4.2	4.0	— 8.5	—1.0	— 1.9
Louisiana	18.8	25.4	— 4.3	— .9	3.8
Mississippi	7.4	4.9	— 9.7	.4	— .4
N. Carolina	16.2	12.0	— 6.0	— .7	.9
Oklahoma	— 3.4	— 6.0	—20.6	— .5	—17.1
S. Carolina	19.3	19.8	— .7	— .4	5.6
Tennessee	14.7	14.8	— 1.9	—1.3	9.4
Texas	22.6	27.1	— 1.2	— .2	4.2
Virginia	28.1	30.3	.6	— .5	8.4

SOURCES: Population data from U.S. Census of 1950, Series P-B and P-C. School attendance figures compiled from data gathered by SSCPEA staff from reports and records of state departments of education.

5. *Negro Population and School Attendance*

Negro school attendance in the South between 1940 and 1950 increased twice as fast as the total Negro population. There were two main reasons: a sharp drop in the infant mortality rate (which resulted in an increased proportion of Negro children reaching school age) and an increase in the proportion of eligible Negro children who actually went to school.

	Per Cent Changes between 1940 and 1950				
	Total Negro Population	Negro Population by Age Groups 5-9	10-14	15-17	Negro School Attendance
South	1.5%				3.3%
Alabama	— .4	.9	— 7.4	—1.5	5.1
Arkansas	—11.6	— 3.9	—15.1	4.2	— 6.3
Florida	17.3	27.1	4.9	.1	20.9
Georgia	— 2.0	.7	— 7.1	.7	1.9
Kentucky	— 5.7	— 2.0	—17.6	2.0	—11.1
Louisiana	3.9	13.4	— 2.1	— .5	9.0
Mississippi	— 8.2	— 1.2	—10.6	— .3	— .4
N. Carolina	10.7	10.9	— 2.7	.6	1.2
Oklahoma	—13.8	—12.1	—23.2	— .7	—16.6
S. Carolina	1.0	7.8	— 2.9	— .7	9.9
Tennessee	4.3	8.7	— 5.8	— .1	4.8
Texas	5.7	4.9	— 9.5	— .7	— 2.4
Virginia	11.0	12.2	— 5.3	.5	9.5

SOURCES: Population data from U.S. Census of 1950, Series P-B and P-C. School attendance figures compiled from data gathered by SSCPEA staff from reports and records of state departments of education.

6. *The South's Public School*

The following table illustrates the magnitude of the South's educational effort in 1952. The data were collected from reports and records of state departments of education and are for expenditures at the local level. The data are not exactly comparable, therefore, to the United States Office of Education statistics which include expenditures for state departments of education, certain lunchroom costs, and other minor items omitted in state reports.

	Current Expenditures		
	Instruction	Transportation	Other
South	$889,141,618	$80,664,198	$249,922,316
Alabama	60,133,367	5,640,985	9,770,815
Arkansas	25,978,154	4,152,820	6,994,424
Florida	68,879,759	3,788,943	15,910,437
Georgia	74,000,828	9,230,177	19,363,035
Kentucky	48,316,962	4,955,369	17,347,924
Louisiana	58,777,684	7,762,687	29,751,900
Mississippi	29,178,809	5,290,008	7,599,274
N. Carolina [2]	90,901,261	6,486,084	27,646,674
Oklahoma	60,983,885 [3]	4,748,796	16,902,930
S. Carolina	44,213,376	1,967,211	12,233,060
Tennessee	60,207,640	6,248,033	18,667,091
Texas	202,077,670	14,951,340	50,993,828
Virginia	65,492,223	5,441,745	16,740,924

SOURCE: Compiled from data gathered by the SSCPEA staff from records and reports of state departments of education.

1. Does not include debt service.
2. 1950-51 data.

Expenditures in 1952

The figures for "Other" in column 4 cover expenditures for administration, operation, maintenance, fixed charges, and auxiliary services such as health service and school lunch. "Capital Outlay" in column 6 means the amount actually spent in 1952. "Debt Service" in column 7 includes interest and payment on principal on bonds and short term loans, and other debt service items. Total current expenditures for Kentucky and Tennessee include special vocational training for veterans.

Total	Capital Outlay	Debt Service	Total Expenditures
$1,219,728,132	$314,905,741	$96,809,606	$1,631,443,479
75,545,167	7,187,373	2,090,959	84,823,499
37,125,398	10,338,240	5,074,001	52,537,639
88,579,139	34,554,771	9,674,500	132,808,410
102,594,040	14,486,866	8,900,704	125,981,610
70,620,255	5,322,710	10,456,108	86,399,073
96,292,271	22,418,131	9,598,238	128,308,640
42,068,091	14,225,525	n.a.	56,293,616 [1]
125,034,019	47,218,108	6,834,622	179,086,749
82,635,611	4,628,107	160,364 [4]	87,424,082
58,413,647	8,136,089	2,708,300	69,258,036
85,122,764	23,067,131	3,100,855	111,290,750
268,022,838	71,881,273	33,845,889 [5]	373,750,000 [5]
87,674,892	51,441,417	4,365,066	143,481,375

3. Includes salaries of teachers, principals, and superintendents only; instructional materials *not* included.

4. Includes interest only.

5. Estimated.

n.a.—not available

7. *Recent Gains in Current Expenditures per Pupil*

From 1940 to 1952, current expenditures per pupil in Southern schools increased more than three-fold. Every state in the South showed a substantial increase, and even discounting the effects of inflation, the rise was considerable. The North Carolina data for 1952 are for the 1950-51 school year.

	1940	1952	Per Cent Gain, 1940-52
The U.S.	$88.09	––	
South	46.98	$163.00	247%
Alabama	34.58	128.61	272
Arkansas	28.95	105.81	272
Florida	57.56	193.01	235
Georgia	40.62	160.92	296
Kentucky	45.75	147.86	223
Louisiana	54.02	217.23	302
Mississippi	29.36	81.71	178
N. Carolina	40.56	153.22	278
Oklahoma	62.95	204.16	224
S. Carolina	38.71	136.70	253
Tennessee	43.54	143.18	229
Texas	66.72	213.34	220
Virginia	47.98	157.46	228

SOURCE: State figures compiled from data gathered by SSCPEA staff from records and reports of state departments of education. U.S. data taken from "Statistics of State School Systems," *Biennial Survey of Education*, U.S. Office of Education.

8. Current Expenditures per Pupil for White and Negro Children

The following table illustrates one aspect of the progress which the South has made in recent years to close the gap between white and Negro education. It also indicates the magnitude of the gap in white-Negro current expenditures which still remained in 1952.

Transportation costs are normally included in current expenditures, because they are part of the cost of operating a school system. However, they are *not* included in this table and in the following two tables, because they tend to distort comparisons of the quality of education. For example, high transportation costs do not necessarily mean better education. The figures for the South are estimates for the thirteen Southern states, since the data cover only nine states. The 1952 figures for North Carolina are for the school year 1950-51.

	1940		1952		Negro as % of White	
	White	Negro	White	Negro	1940	1952
South	$50.14	$21.54	$164.83	$115.08	43%	70%
Alabama	41.38	13.85	127.72	102.25	33	80
Arkansas	30.10	13.01	102.05	67.75	43	66
Florida	62.78	27.36	195.01	153.24	44	79
Georgia	46.70	14.61	163.76	110.59	31	68
Louisiana	63.59	20.33	n. a.	n. a.	32	—
Mississippi	41.71	7.24	117.43	35.27	17	30
N. Carolina	41.69	27.30	152.20	128.67	65	85
Oklahoma	59.10	62.81	n. a.	n. a.	106	—
S. Carolina	50.81	15.16	159.34	95.65	30	60

Source: Compiled and derived from data gathered by SSCPEA from records and reports of state departments of education.
n.a.—not available

9. *Current Expenditures per Pupil in Metropolitan and Rural Districts*

The following table illustrates one aspect of the progress which the South has made in closing the gap between school expenditures in metropolitan areas and rural areas. In most states the gap had been narrowed percentagewise, and in one or two states it had been closed. The progress varied from state to state, and in at least two states, the gap had widened. Moreover, there was still a substantial gap, dollarwise, in 1952.

Transportation costs are not included in the figures. The figures for metropolitan districts cover all such districts in the South except in Texas, where a directed sample was used and in Kentucky, where only two metropolitan districts were included. The figures for rural districts are based on a directed sample in all states except South Carolina, where all rural districts were covered. The 1952 figures for North Carolina are for the 1950-51 school year.

	Metropolitan Districts		Rural Districts		Rural as Per Cent of Metropolitan	
	1940	1952	1940	1952	1940	1952
South	$53.89	$178.23	$32.98	$133.40	61%	75%
Alabama	40.70	131.59	27.11	110.32	67	84
Arkansas	43.80	129.35	20.54	91.80	47	71
Florida	61.13	199.71	53.67	169.86	88	85
Georgia	56.73	169.40	30.23	129.23	53	76
Kentucky	83.28	265.75	n. a.	116.39	—	44
Louisiana	63.14	233.31	44.80	178.79	71	77
Mississippi	34.80	119.85	20.70	56.46	59	47
N. Carolina	44.51	167.34	34.75	130.97	78	78
Oklahoma	n. a.	206.56	n. a.	189.07	—	92
S. Carolina	45.24	150.40	29.92	114.30	66	76
Tennessee	54.68	154.69	32.39	125.74	59	81
Texas	n. a.	204.30	n. a.	211.73	—	104
Virginia	64.80	184.77	35.70	109.54	55	59

SOURCE: Compiled and derived from data gathered by SSCPEA staff from records and reports of state departments of education.
n.a.—not available

10. Current Expenditures per Pupil in White and Negro Schools of Metropolitan and Rural Districts, 1952

The following table points up the fact that the disparity between white and Negro education in the South is much greater in rural areas than in metropolitan areas. It also gives additional insight into the urban-rural gap, since it shows that in some states expenditures for Negro children in metropolitan districts are higher than expenditures for white children in rural areas. The figures in this table were compiled in the same manner as those in Table 9 and do not reflect transportation costs.

	Metropolitan Districts		Rural Districts		Negro as % of White	
	White	Negro	White	Negro	Met.	Rural
Seven States	$166.32	$126.45	$138.24	$ 85.10	76%	62%
Alabama	147.20	105.40	122.14	96.41	72	79
Arkansas	135.74	111.58	97.71	67.24	82	69
Florida	204.58	179.54	189.51	119.22	88	63
Georgia	184.57	132.66	147.34	89.79	72	61
Mississippi	152.30	78.11	82.73	27.05	51	33
N. Carolina	169.64	161.14	148.98	117.23	95	79
S. Carolina	170.21	116.75	179.31	78.77	69	44

SOURCE: Derived from data gathered by SSCPEA staff from records and reports of state departments of education.

11. *Capital Outlays per Pupil for White and Negro Schools*

Another measure of the progress which the South has made in closing the white-Negro gap in education is the fact that capital outlays
for Negro schools increased at far faster rate than outlays for white
schools between 1940 and 1952. However, the gap was still substantial,
dollarwise, in 1952. Because capital outlays fluctuate from year to
year, comparisons among states and between years have certain limitations. However, the following table does provide an indication of the
overall trend. The 1952 figures for North Carolina are for the school
year 1950-51.

	1940		1952		Negro as % of White	
	White	Negro	White	Negro	1940	1952
Eight States	$4.37	$ .99	$36.25	$29.58	23	82
Alabama	6.68	.62	14.19	8.55	10	60
Arkansas	3.20	.70	5.48	3.24	22	59
Florida	6.39	.80	74.03	79.18	13	107
Georgia	2.14	.23	26.80	14.28	17	53
Mississippi	n. a.	n. a.	25.48	35.23	—	138
N. Carolina	6.04	1.84	59.10	54.90	30	93
Oklahoma	1.49	3.86	n. a.	n. a.	259	—
S. Carolina	6.25	.66	24.70	11.45	11	46

SOURCE: Compiled and derived from data gathered by SSCPEA staff from
reports and records of state departments of education.
n.a.—not available

12. *Length of the School Year*

Another measure of the progress which the South has been making in public education in recent years is the increasing length of the school year. Every one of the states covered in the following table which had a gap between the length of the white and Negro school years in 1940 had either completely closed it or significantly narrowed it by 1952. Moreover, in all but three states—two of which were already higher than the twelve-state median average—the length of the school year in white schools was increased.

| | Average Number of Days in the School Year | | | | | |
| | 1940 | | 1950 | | 1952 | |
	White	Negro	White	Negro	White	Negro
Median, 12 states	166	160	178	176	178	177
Alabama	157	147	176	177	176	176
Arkansas	163	144	175	169	172	171
Florida	169	164	180	180	180	180
Georgia	166[1]	157[1]	180	176	180	180
Kentucky[1]	158	170	171	176	172	178
Louisiana	180	144	180	171	179	174
Mississippi	160	124	160	141	167	158
N. Carolina	164	164	180	180	180[2]	180[2]
S. Carolina	175	147	180	174	180	178
Tennessee	166[1]	167[1]	176	176	176	176
Texas	174	162	175	175	175	175
Virginia	180	180	180	180	180	180

SOURCE: Compiled from data gathered by SSCPEA staff from records and reports of state departments of education. (Oklahoma figures not available.)

1. Calculated by dividing aggregate days in attendance by average daily attendance, since state average was not available. All other figures are taken directly from annual reports or records in state departments of education.

2. 1950-51 data.

13. *Training of Classroom Teachers*

By 1952, the gap between the average number of years of college training received by white and Negro teachers in the South had been virtually closed. As a matter of fact, in four of the twelve reporting states (Kentucky data were not available) the Negro teachers averaged more years of college training than the white teachers, and in a fifth the averages were identical. The number of years of college training received by white teachers also increased in most of the reporting states.

| | Average Years of College Training Received by Classroom Teachers | | | | | |
| | 1940 | | 1950 | | 1952 | |
	White	Negro	White	Negro	White	Negro
Average for 12 Southern States	3.4	2.7	3.6	3.3	3.8	3.5
Alabama	3.2	2.1	3.3	3.0	4.1	3.4
Arkansas	2.4	2.0	[1]	[1]	3.4	3.1
Florida	[1]	[1]	4.0	3.8	4.2	4.0
Georgia	3.0	1.7	3.3	3.2	3.6	3.7
Louisiana	3.4	2.4	3.7	3.2	3.8	3.6
Mississippi	3.5	1.5	3.5	1.2	3.7	1.9
N. Carolina [2]	3.9	3.5	3.8	4.0	3.9[3]	4.1[3]
Oklahoma	3.7	3.6	3.9	4.0	4.1	4.1
S. Carolina	[1]	[1]	3.6	3.0	3.7	3.4
Tennessee	2.8	2.6	2.9	3.3	3.3	3.6
Texas	3.7	3.3	4.0	4.0	4.2	4.1
Virginia	3.4	3.1	3.3	3.6	3.4	3.7

SOURCE: Compiled by SSCPEA staff from reports and records of state departments of education.

1. Not available.
2. Supervisors, principals and classroom teachers.
3. 1950-51 data.

14. *Salaries of Classroom Teachers*

Since teachers' salaries are geared to the amount of college training they have received, the gap between the salaries of white and Negro teachers in the South has been closing at about the same pace as the gap between the relative amounts of training. (See Table 13.) In three of the twelve reporting states, the average salary of Negro teachers in 1952 was higher than that for white teachers, reflecting the fact that they had more training, and in a fourth state the salaries and relative amounts of training were about equal. In some states, however, the dollar gap was considerable. Except where noted, the figures are based on a directed sample of rural counties, and on all metropolitan counties in each state except Texas, where a directed sample was used.

	Average Annual Salaries of Classroom Teachers					
	1940		1952		1940	1952
	White	Negro	White	Negro	Negro as % of White	
12 Southern States	$ 894	$487	$2,740	$2,389	54%	87%
Alabama	848	402	2,541	2,359	47	93
Arkansas	626	368	1,929	1,524	59	79
Florida	1,116	577	3,195	2,922	52	91
Georgia	863	390	2,599	2,410	45	93
Louisiana	1,047	390	3,095	2,666	37	86
Mississippi	776[1]	232[1]	1,991	1,019	30	51
N. Carolina[2]	988	717	2,859[3]	2,935[3]	73	103
Oklahoma	998	971	2,978	2,985	97	100
S. Carolina	938	388	2,644	1,985	43	75
Tennessee	858	651	2,141	2,244	76	105
Texas	1,120	681	3,204	3,078	61	96
Virginia	987[1]	605[1]	2,512	2,577	61	103

SOURCE: Except as noted below, figures compiled by SSCPEA staff from reports and records of state departments of education.

1. From *Biennial Survey of Education.* Includes supervisors, principals, and classroom teachers.

2. Supervisors, principals, and classroom teachers.

3. 1950-51 data.

15. *Number of Books in School Libraries*

One of the gaps between white and Negro education in the South which has remained wide is the disparity between the number of books in the libraries of white and Negro schools. Although substantial progress had been made toward closing this gap by 1950, the number of books per pupil in the libraries of Negro schools in the five reporting states was considerably less than half of the figure for white schools.

	Number of Volumes in School Libraries per Pupil Enrolled		Per Cent Change
	1940	1950	1940-1950
Georgia			
White	3.0	4.8	+ 60%
Negro	0.5	1.5	+200
Total	2.1	3.7	+ 76
Louisiana			
White	3.2	5.4	+ 69
Negro	0.5	1.9	+280
Total	2.2	4.1	+ 86
North Carolina			
White	3.0	5.4	+ 47
Negro	1.2	2.4	+100
Total	2.4	4.5	+ 88
South Carolina			
White	2.3	3.0	+ 30
Negro	0.7	0.9	+ 29
Total	1.6	2.0	+ 25
Texas			
White	3.9	4.4	+ 13
Negro	0.9	2.1	+133
Total	3.4	4.0	+ 18
Total for 5 states			
White	3.3	4.7	+ 42
Negro	0.8	1.8	+125
Total	2.5	3.8	+ 52

SOURCE: Compiled from data gathered by SSCPEA staff from records of state departments of education.

II. POPULATION

DURING THE 1940-1950 DECADE, THERE WERE SIGNIFICANT changes in the South's population. To begin with, the total population of the South increased, but not as fast as the total population of the rest of the United States. Secondly, the South's white population increased at a much faster rate than its Negro population. Thirdly, there was a definite shift of Negro population away from the South to the industrial areas of the North and West. And finally, there was also a shift of population from the rural areas of the South to the urban areas of the South. These changes are illustrated in Tables 16 through 22.

During the past half-century, the South's Negro population as a percentage of its total population has declined steadily, both in the large cities and in rural areas. This long-run change is illustrated in Tables 23 and 24.

16. *Recent Changes in the South's Total Population*

From 1940 to 1950, the total population of the South increased by 12.7 per cent, but this was less than the increase in the population of the United States as a whole, and less than the increase in the population of the non-South. Within the South, the state-by-state population change ranged all the way from a 4.4 per cent loss in Oklahoma to a 46 per cent gain in Florida.

	Total Population		1940-50 Change	
	1940	1950	Number	Per Cent
The U.S.	131,669,275	150,697,361	19,028,086	14.5%
U.S. except South	94,656,188	108,969,089	14,312,901	15.1
The South	37,013,087	41,728,272	4,715,185	12.7
Alabama	2,832,961	3,061,743	228,782	8.1
Arkansas	1,949,387	1,909,511	— 39,876	—2.0
Florida	1,897,414	2,771,305	873,891	46.0
Georgia	3,123,723	3,444,578	320,855	10.3
Kentucky	2,845,627	2,944,806	99,179	3.5
Louisiana	2,363,880	2,683,516	319,636	13.5
Mississippi	2,183,796	2,178,914	— 4,882	— .2
N. Carolina	3,571,623	4,061,929	490,306	13.7
Oklahoma	2,336,434	2,233,351	—103,083	—4.4
S. Carolina	1,899,804	2,117,027	217,223	11.4
Tennessee	2,915,841	3,291,718	375,877	12.9
Texas	6,414,824	7,711,194	1,296,370	20.2
Virginia	2,677,773	3,318,680	640,907	23.9

SOURCE: U.S. Census, 1950, Series P-B.

17. Recent Changes in the South's White Population

Between 1940 and 1950, the white population of the South increased more than the white population of the United States as a whole and more than the white population of the non-South. The white population of the non-South, as a percentage of the total white population of the United States, declined from 76.6 per cent to 76.1 per cent while the white population of the South, as a percentage of the total white population of the United States, increased from 23.4 per cent to 23.9 per cent.

	White Population		1940-50 Change	
	1940	1950	Number	Per Cent
The U.S.	118,214,870	134,942,028	16,727,158	14.1%
U.S. except South	90,563,729	102,729,499	12,165,770	13.4
As per cent of U.S.	*76.6%*	*76.1%*		—
South	27,651,141	32,212,529	4,561,388	16.5
As per cent of U.S.	*23.4%*	*23.9%*		—
Alabama	1,849,097	2,079,591	230,494	12.5
Arkansas	1,466,084	1,481,507	15,423	1.1
Florida	1,381,986	2,166,051	784,065	56.7
Georgia	2,038,278	2,380,577	342,299	16.8
Kentucky	2,631,425	2,742,090	110,665	4.2
Louisiana	1,511,739	1,796,683	284,944	18.8
Mississippi	1,106,327	1,188,632	82,305	7.4
N. Carolina	2,567,635	2,983,121	415,486	16.2
Oklahoma	2,104,228	2,032,526	−71,702	−3.4
S. Carolina	1,084,308	1,293,405	209,097	19.3
Tennessee	2,406,906	2,760,257	353,351	14.7
Texas	5,487,545	6,726,534	1,238,989	22.6
Virginia	2,015,583	2,581,555	565,972	28.1

SOURCE: U.S. Census, 1950, Series P-B.

18. *Recent Changes in the South's Negro Population*

Between 1940 and 1950, the Negro population of the South increased only 1.5 per cent, but the Negro population of the rest of the United States increased 56.6 per cent. In six of the Southern states, Negro population declined during the decade. During the same period, the white population of the South increased thirty-three times as much as the Negro population. (See Table 17.)

	Negro Population		1940-50 Change	
	1940	1950	Number	Per Cent
The U.S.	12,865,518	15,042,286	2,176,768	16.9%
U.S. except South	3,603,726	5,642,119	2,038,393	56.6
As per cent of U.S.	*28.0%*	*37.5%*		——
South	9,261,792	9,400,167	138,375	1.5
As per cent of U.S.	*72.0%*	*62.5%*		——
Alabama	983,290	979,617	— 3,673	— .4
Arkansas	482,578	426,639	—55,939	—11.6
Florida	514,198	603,101	88,903	17.3
Georgia	1,084,927	1,062,762	—22,165	— 2.0
Kentucky	214,031	201,921	—12,110	— 5.7
Louisiana	849,303	882,428	33,125	3.9
Mississippi	1,074,578	986,494	—88,084	— 8.2
N. Carolina	981,298	1,047,353	66,055	10.7
Oklahoma	168,849	145,503	—23,346	—13.8
S. Carolina	814,164	822,077	7,913	1.0
Tennessee	508,736	530,603	21,867	4.3
Texas	924,391	977,458	53,067	5.7
Virginia	661,449	734,211	72,762	11.0

SOURCE: U.S. Census, 1950, Series P-B.

19. *Recent Changes in the South's Urban and Rural Population*

During the decade 1940-1950, the South was becoming "urbanized" at a much faster rate than the rest of the United States, but at the end of the decade it was still not as "urbanized" as the non-South. The South's urban population (persons living in cities or towns of 2500 or more population) increased 39.1 per cent during the decade, as against 15.4 per cent for the rest of the United States, but at the end of the decade the South's urban population was only 42.9 per cent of its total population, as compared to 65.2 per cent for the rest of the United States. The degree of "urbanization" within the South varied widely from state to state, ranging from a high of 58.4 per cent in Texas to a low of 16.1 per cent in Kentucky.

	Per Cent Change, 1940-50			Per Cent Urban	
	Urban Population	Rural Farm Population	Rural Non-Farm Population	1940	1950
The U.S.	19.5%	—23.6%	43.2%	56.5%	59.0%
U.S. except South	15.4	—19.6	42.0	65.0	65.2
South	39.1	—27.4	45.5	35.1	42.9
Alabama	43.5	—28.2	36.7	30.2	40.1
Arkansas	42.9	—27.8	20.7	22.2	32.3
Florida	49.8	—22.6	76.3	55.1	56.5
Georgia	28.7	—29.4	60.3	34.4	40.1
Kentucky	16.1	—22.6	33.3	29.8	33.5
Louisiana	39.1	—33.3	41.0	41.5	50.8
Mississippi	39.0	—21.6	36.7	19.8	27.6
N. Carolina	27.1	—16.9	53.6	27.3	30.5
Oklahoma	25.9	—40.3	8.1	37.6	49.6
S. Carolina	30.7	—23.3	54.9	24.5	28.8
Tennessee	23.1	—20.1	63.8	35.2	38.4
Texas	58.4	—39.8	33.3	45.4	59.8
Virginia	41.4	—25.6	66.7	35.3	40.3

SOURCE: Calculated from U.S. Census of 1950, Series P-B.

20. *Summary of Recent Changes in the South's Population*

The following table, which summarizes the data in the four preceding tables, shows that the population changes in the thirteen Southern states between 1940 and 1950 have by no means followed a uniform pattern. However, certain generalizations appear to be warranted:

1. In the states where total population increased, the major factor in the increase was a gain in white population.

2. In the states where total population fell off, the major factor in the decrease was a decline in the Negro population.

3. Although the three states with the highest gain in total population (Florida, Virginia, and Texas) also experienced a high degree of urbanization, there appeared to be no close correlation between these two phenomena.

	% Change in Total Population 1940-50	% Change in White Population 1940-50	% Change in Negro Population 1940-50	% Change in Urban Population 1940-50
The U.S.	14.5%	14.1%	16.9%	19.5%
U.S. except South	15.1	13.4	56.6	15.4
South	12.7	16.5	1.5	39.1
Alabama	8.1	12.5	— 0.4	43.5
Arkansas	—2.0	1.1	—11.6	42.9
Florida	46.0	56.7	17.3	49.8
Georgia	10.3	16.8	— 2.0	28.7
Kentucky	3.5	4.2	— 5.7	16.1
Louisiana	13.5	18.8	3.9	39.1
Mississippi	—0.2	7.4	— 8.2	39.0
N. Carolina	13.7	16.2	10.7	27.1
Oklahoma	—4.4	—3.4	—13.8	25.9
S. Carolina	11.4	19.3	1.0	30.7
Tennessee	12.9	14.7	4.3	23.1
Texas	20.2	22.6	5.7	58.4
Virginia	23.9	28.1	11.0	41.4

SOURCE: Tables 16, 17, 18, and 19.

21. *Loss of Southern Population by Migration*

This table illustrates two important points: (1) that the South had lost more than 4 million people to the rest of the country through inter-regional migration as of 1950, and (2) that well over half of this loss was in "non-white" population. (The numerical difference between "non-white" and "Negro" population is very slight. In the South, Negroes represent 98.8 per cent of the non-white population, and in the nation as a whole, 95.5 per cent.)

	White	Non-white	Total
People Born in the South:			
Number Living in the Region in 1950:			
In state of birth	24,286,000	8,300,000	32,586,000
In another Southern state	3,982,000	1,118,000	5,100,000
	28,268,000	9,418,000	37,686,000
Number Living Outside the Region in 1950:	4,651,000	2,693,000	7,344,000
Total Number born in the South	32,919,000	12,111,000	45,030,000
People Living in the South in 1950:			
Number Born in the Region	28,268,000	9,418,000	37,686,000
Number Born Outside the Region	3,028,000	101,000	3,129,000
Total Number Living in the South in 1950	31,296,000	9,519,000	40,815,000
NET LOSS THROUGH INTER-REGIONAL MIGRATION AS OF 1950	−1,623,000	−2,592,000	−4,215,000

SOURCE: U.S. Census of 1950, Special Reports, P-E No. 4 (based on 20 per cent sample). Figures are rounded to the nearest thousand.

22. *The South's Natural Increase and Migration*

Between 1940 and 1950, the South's total population increased 12.7 per cent, while the total population of the rest of the United States increased 15.1 per cent. The difference between the major factors influencing both changes tells an interesting story. In the South, the major factor in the change was a gain of 19.5 per cent by natural increase in population, which was partially *offset* by a *loss* of 6.8 per cent through net migration to other regions. In the rest of the U. S., the natural increase was only 11.4 per cent, but it was *reinforced* by a *gain* of 3.7 per cent through migration from the South. Ten of the thirteen Southern states had losses through net migration.

	Per Cent Net Change in Total Population 1940-1950	Accounted for by:	
		Natural Increase	Net Migration
The U.S.	14.5%	13.7%	0.8%
U.S. except South	15.1	11.4	3.7
South	12.7	19.5	— 6.8
Alabama	8.1	21.0	—12.9
Arkansas	—2.1	20.2	—22.3
Florida	46.1	16.5	29.6
Georgia	10.3	20.6	—10.3
Kentucky	3.5	16.6	—13.1
Louisiana	13.5	20.1	— 6.6
Mississippi	—0.2	20.6	—20.8
N. Carolina	13.7	21.9	— 8.1
Oklahoma	—4.4	14.7	—19.1
S. Carolina	11.4	25.0	—13.6
Tennessee	12.9	19.2	— 6.3
Texas	20.2	19.8	0.4
Virginia	23.9	17.7	6.2

SOURCE: U.S. Department of Commerce, Bureau of Foreign and Domestic Commerce: *Regional Trends in the U.S. Economy.*

23. Long-Range Population Changes in the South's Largest Cities

Although there has been a mass movement of Negroes from the rural areas of the South into the metropolitan areas of the region, the proportion of Negroes in the South's largest cities declined from 1900 to 1950. The major factors contributing to this phenomenon were: (1) the mass migration of Negroes out of the South to Northern industrial centers, part of which was from Southern cities, and (2) the movement of rural whites into the South's large cities. Comparisons between cities, and between time periods in the same city, are subject to qualification because of the uneven expansion of the geographic boundaries of various cities since 1900. Thus, for those cities whose limits in 1950 had not been expanded to include suburbs where white population has grown rapidly, the 1950 percentage of Negroes shown here is higher than it would be if the whole metropolitan population were measured.

	Total Population		Negro Population		Per Cent Negro	
	1900	1950	1900	1950	1900	1950
Alabama:						
Birmingham	38,415	326,037	16,575	130,025	43.1	39.9
Gadsden	4,282	55,725	1,569	10,808	36.6	19.4
Mobile	38,469	129,009	17,045	45,819	44.3	35.5
Montgomery	30,346	106,525	17,229	42,538	56.8	39.9
Arkansas:						
Little Rock	38,307	102,213	14,694	23,517	38.4	23.0
Florida:						
Jacksonville	28,429	204,517	16,236	72,450	52.1	35.4
Miami	1,681	249,276	(e) 439	40,262	26.1	16.2
Orlando	2,481	52,367	(e) 878	13,378	35.4	25.5
St. Petersburg	1,575	96,738	(e) 370	13,977	23.5	14.4
Tampa	15,839	124,681	4,382	27,364	27.7	21.9
Georgia:						
Atlanta	89,872	331,314	35,727	121,285	39.8	36.6
Augusta	39,441	71,508	18,487	29,304	46.9	41.0
Columbus	17,614	79,611	7,267	24,816	41.3	31.2
Macon	23,272	70,252	11,550	29,534	49.6	42.0
Savannah	54,244	119,638	28,090	48,282	51.8	40.4

	Total Population		Negro Population		Per Cent Negro	
	1900	1950	1900	1950	1900	1950
Kentucky:						
Covington	42,938	64,452	2,487	3,574	5.8	5.6
Lexington	26,369	55,534	10,130	13,655	38.4	24.6
Louisville	204,731	389,129	39,139	57,657	19.1	15.6
Louisiana:						
Baton Rouge	11,269	125,629	6,596	35,117	58.5	28.0
New Orleans	287,104	570,445	77,714	181,775	27.1	31.9
Shreveport	16,013	127,206	8,542	42,169	53.3	33.2
Mississippi:						
Jackson	7,816	98,271	4,447	40,168	56.9	40.9
North Carolina:						
Asheville	14,694	53,000	4,724	12,434	32.1	23.5
Charlotte	18,091	134,042	7,151	37,481	39.5	28.0
Durham	6,679	71,311	2,241	26,095	33.6	36.6
Greensboro	10,035	74,389	4,086	19,109	40.7	25.7
Raleigh	13,643	65,679	5,721	17,871	41.9	27.2
Winston-Salem	13,650	87,811	5,531	36,730	40.5	41.8
Oklahoma:						
Oklahoma City	10,037	243,504	1,219	21,006	12.1	8.6
Tulsa	1,390	182,740	(e) 257	17,126	18.5	9.4
South Carolina:						
Charleston	55,807	70,174	31,522	30,854	56.5	44.0
Columbia	21,108	86,914	9,858	31,221	68.5	35.9
Greenville	11,860	58,161	5,414	16,074	45.6	27.6
Tennessee:						
Chattanooga	30,154	131,041	13,122	39,276	43.5	30.0
Knoxville	32,637	124,269	7,359	19,171	22.5	15.4
Memphis	102,320	396,000	49,910	147,141	48.8	37.2
Nashville	80,865	174,307	30,044	54,696	37.2	31.4
Texas:						
Amarillo	1,442	74,246	(e) 12	3,592	0.8	4.8
Austin	22,258	132,459	5,822	17,667	26.2	13.3
Beaumont	9,427	94,014	2,953	27,573	31.3	29.3
Corpus Christi	4,703	108,287	460	7,101	9.8	6.6
Dallas	42,638	434,462	9,035	56,958	21.2	13.1

El Paso	15,906	130,485	466	3,116	2.9	2.4
Fort Worth	26,688	278,778	4,449	36,933	15.9	13.2
Galveston	37,789	66,568	8,291	17,627	21.9	26.5
Houston	44,633	596,163	14,608	124,766	32.7	21.9
Laredo	13,429	51,910	87	74	0.6	0.1
Lubbock	n. a.	71,747	n. a.	6,229	n. a.	8.7
Port Arthur	900	57,530	(e) 249	13,933	27.7	24.2
San Angelo	n. a.	52,093	n. a.	2,985	n. a.	5.7
San Antonio	53,321	408,442	7,538	28,729	14.1	7.0
Waco	20,686	84,706	5,826	14,571	28.2	17.2
Wichita Falls	2,480	68,042	(e) 87	5,910	3.5	8.7

Virginia:

Alexandria	14,528	61,787	4,533	7,622	31.2	12.3
Norfolk	46,624	213,513	20,230	62,826	43.4	29.4
Portsmouth	17,427	80,039	5,625	30,494	32.3	38.1
Richmond	85,050	230,310	32,230	72,996	37.9	31.7
Roanoke	21,495	91,921	5,834	14,575	27.1	15.9

SOURCES: 12th and 17th Censuses of the U.S.

(e)—estimated

n.a.—not available

24. *Population Changes in the South's 1300 Counties*

The following table illustrates the fact that changes in the South's population during the past half-century and the 1940-50 decade varied considerably from county to county. However, the overall decline in Negro population as a percentage of total population, is readily apparent. Although the figures are in terms of white and non-white population, whereas most of the figures in the preceding tables have been in terms of white and Negro population, the disparity is not significant because Negroes in the South make up 98.8 per cent of the non-white population.

Counties are listed as they existed in 1950. A number of counties existing in earlier years had been absorbed by 1950. Italicized counties are predominantly urban—that is, they had 50 per cent or more urban population in 1950. The letters "n.o." signify that the county or independent city had not been established at the time the data was taken. A dash (——) in the columns for 1900 and 1950 signifies that there were less than 0.1 per cent Negroes of the total population of the county at the time of the census. For the column showing per cent change, a dash indicates populations too small (usually less than 100) for the change to be meaningfully expressed in percentage. The subregionalization of all the states excluding Texas and Oklahoma was adapted from data prepared for the Southern Regional Study (see *Social Forces,* Volume 13, No. 1 [October 1934], "The Subregions of the Southeast," by T. J. Woofter, Jr.). The subregionalization of Texas and Oklahoma was adapted from *Rural Regions of the United States,* A. R. Mangus, Division of Research, Works Projects Administration, U. S. Government Printing Office, Washington, D. C., 1940. The assignment of some counties to particular subregions was necessarily arbitrary (as, for example, when county lines were bisected by subregional lines). Also a few counties that had the characteristics of one subregional grouping in earlier years have since experienced sharp ethnic changes, but they are left in the earlier grouping and the change is indicated in part by the data in this table.

	Per Cent Change 1940 to 1950		Non-white as Per Cent of Total	
	White	Non-White	1900	1950
ALABAMA				
Coastal				
Baldwin	31.1	14.0	31.7	22.5
Mobile	69.6	50.9	45.3	33.8
Old Cotton-Tobacco				
Autauga	.4	—25.3	62.4	46.0
Barbour	— 7.5	—15.0	63.6	53.4
Bibb	—10.1	—12.1	33.6	32.4
Bullock	— 2.6	—23.6	81.7	73.6
Butler	— 3.8	—16.5	51.4	44.8
Chilton	— 3.1	— 6.9	19.8	16.0
Choctaw	— 4.0	— 6.2	56.7	52.5
Clarke	1.0	— 8.4	57.0	49.7
Clay	—18.0	—15.6	11.0	15.9
Coffee	— 4.7	— 1.3	20.2	21.1
Conecuh	—15.8	—13.0	44.5	45.3
Coosa	— 8.5	—19.7	32.8	33.4
Covington	— 3.4	—11.9	15.9	15.1
Crenshaw	—18.5	—22.0	28.5	32.0
Dale	— 8.4	— 7.6	23.0	23.3
Dallas	36.0	—10.3	83.0	65.0
Elmore	— 3.2	—16.3	46.2	36.0
Escambia	1.9	3.8	31.1	33.6
Geneva	—11.3	—15.3	16.9	13.2
Greene	— 9.8	—14.9	86.3	83.0
Hale	—13.7	—20.2	81.7	70.3
Henry	—14.6	—15.0	37.6	48.7
Houston	5.7	— 6.4	n. o.	29.4
Lowndes	— 7.0	—22.9	86.6	82.2
Macon	— 2.9	13.5	81.6	84.4
Marengo	— 7.3	—21.3	76.9	69.4
Monroe	— 9.2	—15.8	55.4	51.1
Montgomery	37.3	5.7	72.5	43.6
Perry	—11.5	—27.8	78.5	67.5
Pickens	—12.9	—11.0	57.0	47.9
Pike	— 1.3	—10.9	42.8	44.2
Russell	31.9	— .5	78.1	52.0
Shelby	7.4	— 3.5	29.6	21.8
Sumter	.5	—17.2	82.7	76.1
Talladega	—29.5	10.3	50.9	31.5
Washington	— 5.5	— .4	45.2	39.3
Wilcox	—13.9	— 9.8	80.4	79.1

| | Per Cent Change 1940 to 1950 | | Non-white as Per Cent of Total | |
	White	Non-White	1900	1950
ALABAMA (*Cont.*)				
Uplands				
Blount	— .3	—34.8	7.7	2.8
Calhoun	27.9	16.8	30.5	19.1
Chambers	3.4	—19.2	53.5	36.7
Cherokee	—12.2	— 4.4	14.3	9.4
Cleburne	—12.0	—20.5	6.7	6.6
Colbert	22.4	— 3.0	42.7	21.0
Culiman	3.9	—17.7	0.1	1.0
Etowah	29.6	28.1	16.0	14.4
Fayette	—11.1	— 6.6	12.0	14.8
Franklin	— 6.6	— 8.5	13.1	5.2
Jefferson	24.8	16.4	40.5	37.3
Lamar	—16.3	—18.3	19.1	14.8
Lauderdale	21.1	— 2.9	27.8	13.4
Lawrence	— 1.9	— 5.5	35.6	21.9
Lee	70.1	—12.1	59.9	40.2
Limestone	3.0	— 7.8	43.9	22.8
Madison	10.8	7.7	45.5	27.2
Marion	— 4.5	—27.6	5.4	2.7
Marshall	6.8	—10.3	6.4	2.3
Morgan	12.5	— 2.8	25.6	15.0
Randolph	—15.1	— .8	23.9	25.8
St. Clair	.9	—14.9	17.7	18.2
Tallapoosa	4.2	—10.7	36.0	28.6
Tuscaloosa	31.6	6.9	40.5	27.5
Walker	— .7	— .8	16.4	10.7
Winston	— 2.6	— 8.9	0.1	0.6
Highlands				
DeKalb	4.6	3.5	4.1	1.9
Jackson	— 6.4	—11.8	11.9	5.9
ARKANSAS				
Old Cotton-Tobacco				
Arkansas	— 3.9	— 0.6	31.3	23.3
Ashley	9.8	—20.7	53.7	38.0
Bradley	—10.6	—13.7	34.6	33.7
Calhoun	—29.3	—18.8	38.5	34.4
Chicot	—11.3	—24.1	87.1	54.6
Clark	— 3.0	—12.4	34.1	27.3

Cleveland	—26.3	—35.5	30.2	24.4
Columbia	7.4	—16.7	42.9	39.1
Crittenden	47.5	— 1.1	84.6	66.8
Cross	6.2	—22.2	44.0	32.2
Dallas	—17.4	— 8.7	39.8	39.2
Desha	19.3	—25.4	81.7	48.0
Drew	2.6	—26.4	52.9	33.7
Grant	—13.3	—19.5	11.0	8.2
Hempstead	—20.8	—27.0	49.7	40.8
Howard	—16.2	—31.3	22.0	20.5
Jackson	— 0.9	— 7.9	28.8	14.5
Jefferson	31.2	5.3	72.8	49.8
Lafayette	—17.1	—26.5	61.2	45.2
Lee	0.7	—15.1	77.8	59.4
Lincoln	1.5	—23.2	63.1	53.3
Little River	—23.2	—32.5	41.9	33.7
Lonoke	— 2.4	—23.3	41.2	24.4
Miller	6.7	— 7.9	43.4	27.0
Mississippi	9.2	—11.6	50.8	26.9
Monroe	— 2.7	—12.2	65.4	48.8
Nevada	—24.4	—27.7	35.1	36.0
Ouachita	18.7	— 8.0	55.7	40.9
Phillips	22.3	—10.1	78.6	59.7
Pike	—14.2	—27.0	5.8	4.9
Poinsett	9.3	—30.4	14.7	8.3
Prairie	— 6.7	—24.0	35.3	16.4
Pulaski	32.3	9.5	46.1	24.0
St. Francis	22.0	— 8.8	64.1	57.4
Sevier	—18.8	—26.6	12.5	9.6
Union	3.7	—11.2	43.2	31.9
Woodruff	—10.7	—19.8	61.0	37.6
Highlands				
Baxter	13.6	——	0.1	0.1
Benton	5.4	—16.1	0.4	0.2
Boone	2.5	——	0.9	——
Carroll	—10.2	——	0.9	0.2
Clay	— 6.1	——	0.1	——
Cleburne	—12.6	——	0.1	——
Conway	—14.8	—18.9	38.5	23.6
Craighead	7.7	— 5.2	6.2	3.1
Crawford	— 4.2	—26.2	10.5	2.9
Faulkner	0.2	—18.2	21.4	11.2
Franklin	—20.8	—41.8	3.4	1.6
Fulton	—10.5	——	0.6	0.1
Garland	13.4	10.9	19.6	11.9
Greene	— 3.5	3.6	0.5	0.2
Hot Springs	15.7	28.8	11.6	12.9
Independence	— 8.1	—19.1	6.6	2.8

	Per Cent Change 1940 to 1950		Non-white as Per Cent of Total	
	White	Non-White	1900	1950
ARKANSAS (*Cont.*)				
Izard	—22.4	—27.9	2.1	1.0
Johnson	—14.1	—15.9	3.5	1.5
Lawrence	— 5.8	—18.8	6.4	1.3
Logan	—22.1	—18.1	3.8	2.5
Madison	—19.3	——	0.2	0.1
Marion	— 9.0	——	0.3	——
Montgomery	—24.4	—61.5	3.4	0.5
Newton	—20.2	——	0.1	——
Perry	—28.2	—40.4	11.1	4.1
Polk	—10.5	——	1.0	0.1
Pope	— 8.5	—29.5	8.6	3.1
Randolph	—12.7	—18.3	3.5	1.0
Saline	23.3	43.5	14.6	5.6
Scott	22.8	—70.7	0.8	1.3
Searcy	—12.7	——	0.1	——
Sebastian	3.1	— 9.1	11.9	6.7
Sharp	—21.8	——	1.7	0.1
Stone	—10.9	——	1.0	0.1
Van Buren	—22.7	—19.3	2.9	1.2
Washington	21.7	5.7	2.6	0.9
White	3.3	—18.2	10.7	3.5
Yell	—32.2	—47.4	7.3	3.9
FLORIDA				
Coastal				
Alachua	78.9	3.5	58.8	29.0
Bradford	33.4	25.7	26.5	24.4
Brevard	62.4	13.8	20.8	25.4
Broward	142.3	52.9	n. o.	25.4
Charlotte	20.9	— 0.2	n. o.	15.7
Clay	158.1	21.3	32.5	14.7
Collier	37.3	8.9	n. o.	30.6
Dade	97.2	31.2	26.1	13.2
DeSoto	16.8	25.6	8.4	21.7
Duval	56.9	19.3	56.4	26.9
Flagler	9.8	14.6	n. o.	45.6
Gilchrist	—12.7	—45.8	n. o.	9.9
Glades	—23.1	—14.8	n. o.	40.8
Hardee	— 1.2	3.4	n. o.	7.4
Hendry	32.7	—15.4	n. o.	26.1

Hernando	27.4	— 3.6	49.9	23.0
Highlands	39.3	78.3	n. o.	25.4
Hillsborough	42.5	21.2	23.5	15.3
Indian River	41.7	11.0	n. o.	24.9
Lake	41.4	12.4	35.3	23.5
Lee	38.3	18.6	6.1	20.1
Manatee	39.4	15.0	9.8	22.8
Marion	34.3	6.8	61.7	38.2
Martin	38.6	— 2.2	n. o.	28.2
Monroe	32.2	25.6	32.1	10.8
Nassau	22.5	10.1	52.7	31.3
Okeechobee	15.2	14.7	n. o.	18.6
Orange	73.5	34.4	35.4	19.8
Osceola	23.2	—28.0	12.5	13.1
Palm Beach	54.9	22.5	n. o.	30.3
Pasco	51.7	22.0	27.7	13.5
Pinellas	85.7	15.6	n. o.	11.8
Polk	44.4	38.1	23.6	20.6
Putnam	38.8	9.1	48.3	36.5
St. *Johns*	28.7	17.9	39.5	33.3
St. *Lucie*	76.9	56.7	n. o.	31.7
Sarasota	93.3	28.8	n. o.	16.0
Seminole	29.4	11.0	n. o.	44.4
Sumter	4.0	— 0.9	36.9	26.9
Union	12.8	56.5	n. o.	36.3
Volusia	48.7	10.7	34.6	22.1

Old Cotton-Tobacco

Baker	— 4.7	2.3	26.4	24.5
Bay	115.8	69.7	n. o.	16.8
Calhoun	— 2.5	—10.0	39.8	14.1
Citrus	9.8	— 8.4	48.9	25.4
Columbia	16.8	— 5.9	54.5	33.6
Dixie	—15.3	—81.6	n. o.	14.3
Escambia	53.6	42.5	42.1	22.3
Franklin	8.1	—25.1	45.8	25.7
Gadsden	14.7	16.9	64.4	56.1
Gulf	19.4	—15.9	n. o.	26.9
Hamilton	— 8.3	— 8.0	45.2	42.2
Holmes	— 8.9	—20.5	16.5	4.4
Jackson	4.8	— 6.7	52.5	33.4
Jefferson	— 3.1	—18.7	77.9	62.5
Lafayette	—21.6	—25.1	15.3	9.4
Leon	100.8	26.5	80.4	39.5
Levy	— 8.9	—25.4	38.1	33.9
Liberty	— 8.0	—37.2	50.6	18.3
Madison	— 8.8	—16.2	57.6	45.6
Okaloosa	115.7	90.6	n. o.	8.0
Santa Rosa	20.0	—18.4	24.0	8.5

	Per Cent Change 1940 to 1950		Non-white as Per Cent of Total	
	White	Non-White	1900	1950
FLORIDA (*Cont.*)				
Suwannee	3.6	— 9.2	45.2	29.3
Taylor	— 8.2	—13.7	11.0	30.5
Wakulla	0.4	—11.9	54.2	30.9
Walton	4.2	— 1.9	21.8	13.3
Washington	— 2.7	— 6.5	26.5	17.8
GEORGIA				
Coastal				
Bryan	— 3.6	— 7.5	51.5	39.6
Camden	45.3	8.3	68.4	50.7
Chatham	42.9	10.6	57.9	38.6
Glynn	46.6	8.5	63.6	32.0
Liberty	6.5	— 6.4	65.8	61.2
Long	—10.5	—14.6	n. o.	34.7
McIntosh	9.4	16.3	77.7	61.1
Old Cotton-Tobacco				
Appling	— 3.9	— 1.2	28.5	18.6
Atkinson	— 4.6	— 1.5	n. o.	22.4
Bacon	11.9	0.6	n. o.	11.9
Baker	—24.0	—15.4	71.2	61.0
Baldwin	40.6	3.2	63.3	39.9
Ben Hill	4.5	— 1.7	n. o.	32.0
Berrien	— 7.8	—16.7	30.5	13.9
Bibb	51.8	15.0	54.3	35.8
Bleckley	0.3	—13.7	n. o.	31.1
Brantley	— 2.2	—31.5	n. o.	12.3
Brooks	— 7.2	—15.4	58.6	49.0
Bulloch	— 3.4	— 7.3	42.9	36.9
Burke	1.1	—15.8	81.7	71.3
Butts	1.0	3.4	53.2	45.6
Calhoun	—15.8	—18.8	74.1	67.5
Candler	—12.0	—10.3	n. o.	34.6
Charlton	— 8.6	— 7.5	20.7	28.7
Chattahoochee	—15.3	—37.4	68.0	15.6
Clay	—14.6	—18.4	66.6	69.7
Clinch	— 0.9	—15.8	41.1	35.0
Coffee	12.2	— 7.7	40.9	24.2
Colquitt	4.1	— 0.5	26.4	23.6
Columbia	31.8	—19.5	72.8	47.9

Cook	1.1	5.9	n. o.	27.7
Crawford	—17.2	—12.8	56.1	57.7
Crisp	5.1	— 4.4	n. o.	43.9
Decatur	10.3	1.9	53.6	46.4
Dodge	—11.3	—22.5	40.8	30.3
Dooly	—12.0	—19.5	55.3	53.0
Dougherty	91.3	20.4	82.1	42.9
Early	— 9.6	— 4.1	60.5	52.9
Echols	— 6.9	—31.9	30.9	29.1
Effingham	0.4	—13.5	44.4	37.9
Emanuel	—15.5	—16.5	39.5	35.1
Evans	—14.8	— 0.9	n. o.	37.1
Fayette	— 1.3	— 4.6	35.2	31.9
Glascock	—21.2	—21.5	33.5	26.8
Grady	— 3.3	— 4.6	n. o.	33.9
Greene	— 4.0	— 8.5	67.8	51.0
Hancock	—16.1	—12.4	74.6	72.8
Henry	10.4	— 1.3	50.5	44.6
Houston	240.8	0.9	75.1	35.2
Irwin	— 6.5	— 9.0	34.3	36.1
Jasper	—14.0	—15.5	64.2	56.5
Jeff Davis	1.8	20.4	n. o.	20.9
Jefferson	— 6.7	— 5.4	63.6	57.5
Jenkins	—10.3	—15.8	n. o.	53.6
Johnson	—18.2	—32.5	39.7	33.6
Jones	4.4	—18.4	70.7	55.0
Lamar	7.1	— 5.7	n. o.	40.7
Lanier	—12.0	0.1	n. o.	31.4
Laurens	— 0.2	— 3.2	43.8	40.2
Lee	1.2	—20.0	85.4	71.3
Lincoln	— 3.5	—12.8	59.7	48.9
Lowndes	21.3	— 2.2	53.3	40.8
McDuffie	12.5	— 2.4	62.7	45.3
Macon	— 4.7	—13.7	69.5	66.1
Marion	—14.9	0.9	58.0	59.2
Meriwether	0.0	— 8.5	59.2	50.9
Miller	— 6.2	—18.2	42.9	29.8
Mitchell	1.8	— 7.6	54.1	50.3
Monroe	12.5	—13.0	67.0	50.9
Montgomery	—18.8	—17.5	41.0	40.5
Morgan	— 3.8	— 8.7	67.1	52.0
Newton	11.0	4.1	48.7	33.1
Oconee	— 2.5	—19.3	51.3	26.0
Oglethorpe	—18.6	—21.5	68.5	43.3
Peach	12.9	12.7	n. o.	61.3
Pierce	— 6.8	— 2.0	27.0	21.6
Pike	—13.8	—23.4	51.2	45.9
Pulaski	1.5	—18.4	59.7	49.6
Putnam	0.6	—15.8	74.9	55.5

	Per Cent Change 1940 to 1950		Non-white as Per Cent of Total	
	White	Non-White	1900	1950
GEORGIA (Cont.)				
Quitman	— 3.8	—16.0	73.3	66.3
Randolph	— 0.9	—20.7	67.1	65.5
Richmond	48.6	—10.3	48.9	33.8
Rockdale	13.4	1.3	41.2	29.3
Schley	—17.9	—21.1	65.2	59.3
Screven	—10.3	—12.6	56.9	56.4
Seminole	— 3.3	—12.2	n. o.	38.4
Spalding	15.5	— 4.4	52.0	27.5
Stewart	—12.3	—13.6	74.7	72.5
Sumter	14.6	—11.3	71.8	55.0
Talbot	— 5.3	— 5.7	70.0	69.7
Taliaferro	—17.7	—30.6	69.8	65.8
Tattnall	— 2.0	— 1.7	34.8	25.7
Taylor	—14.9	—15.9	51.0	47.8
Telfair	—13.7	—10.6	40.9	32.4
Terrell	— 0.3	—19.6	70.2	67.2
Thomas	15.8	— 0.7	56.2	40.9
Tift	23.9	16.7	n. o.	28.3
Toombs	1.3	5.8	n. o.	27.5
Treutlen	—14.1	—15.6	n. o.	29.7
Turner	— 6.2	1.9	n. o.	37.0
Twiggs	— 2.7	—12.3	66.6	61.9
Upson	6.2	13.7	54.7	26.4
Ware	9.1	6.6	37.1	26.5
Warren	— 5.6	—15.9	66.5	63.9
Washington	—12.1	—14.1	61.7	56.7
Wayne	10.8	0.5	23.6	19.7
Webster	—19.7	— 9.8	62.2	63.9
Wheeler	—22.6	—18.6	n. o.	32.5
Wilcox	—15.7	—27.7	37.9	34.7
Wilkes	— 9.2	—23.7	69.2	55.7
Wilkinson	—10.3	—12.3	52.7	48.5
Worth	—12.7	— 5.7	45.1	48.6
Uplands				
Banks	—19.1	—39.0	19.9	5.8
Barrow	1.5	— 4.4	n. o.	17.9
Bartow	10.8	— 4.6	29.7	14.7
Carroll	2.1	— 8.3	18.9	19.5
Catoosa	24.8	— 1.2	8.3	2.1
Chatooga	15.0	8.3	17.3	9.3

Clarke	45.2	— 1.3	53.5	27.2
Clayton	120.0	27.1	41.9	16.6
Cobb	73.8	— 0.9	29.7	10.1
Coweta	7.3	— 3.4	56.9	37.6
DeKalb	67.2	3.2	33.4	10.6
Douglas	29.3	— 8.7	24.6	16.3
Elbert	4.0	—19.5	49.6	33.5
Floyd	12.9	7.5	34.7	14.8
Forsyth	— 2.9	—	9.4	0.5
Franklin	— 5.4	—20.3	23.8	12.5
Fulton	21.7	17.9	38.8	30.7
Gwinnett	13.7	— 8.5	16.2	9.4
Hall	15.0	17.4	15.8	9.8
Haralson	4.3	—17.1	13.7	8.6
Harris	5.7	— 6.3	67.7	56.6
Hart	— 5.4	— 9.9	27.8	24.6
Heard	—14.8	—28.7	35.9	26.5
Jackson	— 3.0	—16.9	31.6	15.5
Madison	— 8.5	—10.4	29.4	19.1
Muscogee	76.3	18.3	52.3	26.1
Paulding	— 8.9	— 3.8	10.4	10.6
Polk	9.7	4.2	27.5	16.0
Stephens	30.3	16.7	n. o.	13.0
Troup	22.6	— 1.5	63.9	32.3
Walker	24.6	4.0	15.7	6.1
Walton	— 1.6	— 4.8	39.8	31.1
Whitfield	34.0	— 2.7	12.6	4.1

Highlands

Cherokee	3.6	— 8.3	8.4	4.0
Dade	5.1	— 4.4	9.6	2.1
Dawson	—15.9	—	3.1	—
Fannin	3.0	—	2.6	0.5
Gilmer	21.7	17.9	0.8	0.2
Gordon	3.4	— 9.5	11.6	5.8
Habersham	13.0	— 7.5	13.2	3.7
Lumpkin	7.2	—37.3	6.5	2.1
Murray	— 2.4	—54.1	6.0	1.6
Pickens	— 2.4	—16.1	4.8	4.6
Rabun	— 4.6	—31.1	2.9	1.3
Towns	— 2.6	—	1.5	0.1
Union	— 4.6	—	1.5	—
White	— 7.4	— 5.2	10.1	5.8

KENTUCKY

Old Cotton-Tobacco

Fulton	— 8.4	—23.2	24.6	17.1
Hickman	—15.9	— 7.1	18.1	12.1

	Per Cent Change 1940 to 1950		Non-white as Per Cent of Total	
	White	Non-White	1900	1950
KENTUCKY (Cont.)				
Uplands				
Adair	— 4.5	—15.5	10.7	5.3
Allen	—10.5	—31.3	7.5	1.8
Anderson	1.0	— 7.4	9.9	5.2
Ballard	— 8.0	—31.6	14.0	6.2
Barren	5.7	—18.6	16.3	7.8
Bath	— 7.7	—28.8	11.5	5.2
Boone	22.1	—41.1	7.3	1.4
Bourbon	1.9	—14.6	37.6	15.4
Boyle	26.1	— 9.3	34.6	12.5
Bracken	— 8.5	—40.8	4.7	1.6
Breckenridge	—12.4	—15.5	10.2	4.3
Bullitt	—16.8	— 6.4	11.4	2.5
Butler	—20.9	—44.5	4.6	1.3
Caldwell	— 6.5	—31.0	19.1	7.7
Calloway	6.9	—14.9	7.1	4.0
Campbell	6.1	— 6.0	1.1	1.3
Carlisle	—17.9	—52.3	6.3	1.7
Carroll	— 1.2	—14.2	8.2	3.1
Casey	—11.7	—	3.3	0.4
Christian	29.0	— 9.8	43.7	23.4
Clark	9.5	—23.3	31.0	9.9
Clinton	3.2	—	2.2	0.5
Crittenden	—10.0	—45.6	5.8	1.2
Cumberland	—21.6	—26.0	10.3	6.2
Daviess	11.2	—16.4	14.4	5.1
Edmonson	—17.4	—16.9	4.5	1.4
Fayette	33.9	4.5	36.6	17.3
Fleming	— 9.2	—35.8	9.3	3.0
Franklin	11.0	13.7	20.9	9.5
Gallatin	— 7.2	—26.6	10.9	2.6
Garrard	— 5.0	—25.7	24.5	9.3
Grant	0.0	—46.2	3.2	0.8
Graves	— 0.5	—12.6	10.1	5.6
Grayson	— 2.7	—20.8	2.2	0.5
Green	— 7.9	—17.6	14.2	6.6
Hancock	—11.2	—25.2	7.2	3.1
Hardin	69.8	143.2	9.0	5.8
Harrison	— 7.8	—30.4	13.0	4.8

Hart	—11.3	— 9.2	12.1	9.5
Henderson	19.0	—15.5	26.8	11.5
Henry	— 6.0	—14.7	13.2	7.6
Hopkins	5.2	—16.2	16.5	9.5
Jefferson	26.2	22.5	18.9	12.9
Jessamine	6.6	—26.3	28.1	9.4
Kenton	11.9	13.2	5.2	3.8
Larue	3.4	4.8	7.3	5.5
Lincoln	— 3.8	—32.2	20.6	5.6
Livingston	—20.6	—50.5	6.9	1.5
Logan	— 1.2	—23.2	25.9	11.4
Lyon	—21.7	—41.3	20.7	10.7
McCracken	3.9	—14.5	25.3	12.2
McLean	—11.4	—63.5	7.0	1.0
Madison	13.7	—22.1	26.1	8.8
Marion	2.4	— 4.7	17.3	8.0
Marshall	—18.7	—	2.5	0.1
Mason	— 2.0	—11.9	18.4	10.0
Meade	7.5	11.5	8.4	3.4
Mercer	2.1	—20.6	17.1	6.9
Metcalfe	— 8.6	—21.1	10.0	4.3
Monroe	— 1.6	—18.7	5.2	2.7
Montgomery	9.9	—19.2	27.1	10.1
Muhlenberg	—12.7	—26.2	10.4	5.0
Nelson	10.1	— 7.4	20.8	8.2
Nicholas	—10.9	—40.1	11.1	3.9
Ohio	13.9	41.6	5.1	1.9
Oldham	4.2	— 7.2	22.9	11.0
Owen	—11.9	—10.2	8.4	4.2
Pendleton	— 6.9	—44.8	3.3	1.0
Pulaski	— 3.5	— 3.8	4.3	2.0
Robertson	—15.7	—	2.6	1.1
Russell	1.4	—35.8	3.0	1.1
Scott	9.6	—16.2	28.0	11.8
Shelby	2.5	— 9.1	25.6	13.0
Simpson	1.5	—13.0	21.9	12.9
Spencer	— 7.5	—26.5	16.9	5.7
Taylor	7.5	— 7.6	14.8	7.4
Todd	— 3.7	—29.0	35.5	17.7
Trigg	—22.7	—32.1	24.8	14.9
Trimble	— 8.0	—	2.8	0.2
Union	—11.8	—34.1	14.6	9.3
Warren	20.1	— 5.9	23.3	10.4
Washington	— 1.8	1.7	13.4	10.2
Wayne	— 4.2	— 4.3	4.1	2.7
Webster	—15.0	—43.6	11.9	9.8
Woodford	— 3.1	—16.3	35.9	15.0

	Per Cent Change 1940 to 1950		Non-white as Per Cent of Total	
	White	Non-White	1900	1950
KENTUCKY (Cont.)				
Highlands				
Bell	8.9	1.4	11.2	3.4
Boyd	8.8	3.6	4.1	1.8
Breathitt	—16.5	—35.2	2.1	0.4
Carter	—11.7	——	0.7	0.1
Clay	— 3.7	20.6	3.7	2.1
Elliott	—18.7	——	——	——
Estill	—18.3	—32.4	1.9	0.5
Floyd	1.7	—36.4	0.9	1.2
Greenup	— 0.1	0.0	1.8	0.7
Harlan	— 2.1	—27.7	2.3	7.6
Jackson	—19.7	——	0.2	——
Johnson	— 7.4	——	——	——
Knott	2.1	—40.7	1.9	0.8
Knox	— 1.7	—16.1	4.3	1.7
Laurel	0.9	—17.7	3.7	1.1
Lawrence	—16.5	——	0.9	0.5
Lee	—19.2	——	3.4	0.4
Leslie	3.8	——	1.1	0.1
Letcher	— 0.5	—42.3	0.5	3.0
Lewis	—13.8	——	1.0	0.2
McCreary	1.3	——	n. o.	0.2
Magoffin	—20.8	——	1.1	0.1
Martin	6.4	——	0.3	——
Menifee	—15.7	——	0.6	0.4
Morgan	—19.0	——	0.4	——
Owsley	—18.2	——	1.1	0.5
Perry	— 1.6	—25.7	1.9	3.3
Pike	14.0	17.9	0.8	1.5
Powell	—10.4	—36.9	5.8	2.1
Rockcastle	—18.8	——	1.3	0.1
Rowan	— 0.2	——	0.7	0.1
Whitley	— 3.3	—48.8	3.1	0.6
Wolfe	—23.9	——	1.1	0.1
LOUISIANA				
Coastal				
East Baton Rouge	93.3	55.6	66.1	33.1
Jefferson	109.4	89.3	41.0	15.7
Livingston	12.9	12.0	14.1	14.7

Orleans	12.5	22.6	27.1	32.0
Plaquemines	27.2	1.0	55.8	38.7
St. Bernard	61.7	13.8	43.7	14.6
St. Charles	7.0	11.6	67.3	32.6
St. Helena	— 5.9	— 5.2	54.1	53.1
Tangipahoa	20.2	10.3	30.5	31.2
Old Cotton-Tobacco				
Acadia	0.3	8.2	20.5	19.1
Allen	10.0	0.0	n. o.	24.2
Ascension	9.1	— 0.4	50.0	35.4
Assumption	— 8.7	— 4.0	43.7	41.8
Avoyelles	— 2.0	— 6.1	40.0	26.1
Beauregard	18.5	15.9	n. o.	17.0
Bienville	—22.1	—18.1	46.9	49.2
Bossier	59.0	—16.5	78.2	34.7
Caddo	27.5	4.1	68.9	37.6
Calcasieu	66.2	37.6	19.6	23.0
Caldwell	—14.0	—16.0	44.5	28.5
Cameron	—13.4	—13.0	14.6	9.3
Catahoula	—17.1	—22.4	41.5	35.1
Claiborne	— 5.2	—24.2	60.0	51.7
Concordia	22.6	—12.7	87.4	59.3
DeSoto	3.0	—31.3	67.4	56.6
East Carroll	1.7	—22.1	91.6	61.1
East Feliciana	25.2	— 4.4	72.7	58.2
Evangeline	2.4	8.0	n. o.	23.9
Franklin	— 5.8	—14.7	56.5	36.7
Grant	— 9.6	—13.1	28.4	24.2
Iberia	14.1	— 3.5	49.2	32.4
Iberville	1.1	— 7.9	63.5	48.9
Jackson	—11.1	—18.2	35.1	29.8
Jefferson Davis	13.4	— 5.5	n. o.	21.6
Lafayette	40.8	11.6	41.7	27.2
Lafourche	11.9	— 4.7	28.3	13.5
LaSalle	17.8	3.7	n. o.	11.2
Lincoln	13.8	— 7.8	42.5	40.2
Madison	4.2	— 9.6	92.7	66.2
Morehouse	45.2	— 4.3	76.5	48.2
Natchitoches	0.1	—14.4	58.8	44.9
Ouachita	31.2	17.3	62.5	33.0
Pointe Coupee	— 3.2	—13.5	74.4	53.7
Rapides	30.3	11.8	53.6	33.2
Red River	—23.2	—24.3	64.7	50.0
Richland	— 0.2	—16.3	71.0	41.0
Sabine	—11.9	— 9.7	19.5	20.6
St. James	— 8.9	— 6.3	56.2	50.3
St. John The Baptist	— 5.7	7.9	58.3	49.9
St. Landry	15.4	3.5	50.4	44.6

	Per Cent Change 1940 to 1950		Non-white as Per Cent of Total	
	White	Non-White	1900	1950
LOUISIANA (Cont.)				
St. Martin	— 0.8	1.0	46.9	37.0
St. Mary	28.9	— 3.9	59.3	38.3
St. Tammany	16.8	8.5	36.7	29.4
Tensas	— 2.1	—23.5	93.5	64.8
Terrebonne	25.6	8.0	42.2	24.6
Union	— 8.5	— 8.8	37.6	34.6
Vermilion	— 1.5	— 6.8	18.1	12.7
Vernon	0.2	— 8.4	12.4	11.7
Washington	11.3	11.6	28.8	31.5
Webster	16.7	— 8.6	54.6	36.5
West Baton Rouge	24.8	— 9.0	77.1	53.2
West Carroll	— 5.8	—26.6	57.7	18.1
West Feliciana	5.9	—19.2	86.2	71.2
Winn	— 7.5	3.2	17.4	27.4
MISSISSIPPI				
Coastal				
George	17.6	— 0.7	n. o.	12.3
Greene	—10.9	—24.2	26.2	18.3
Hancock	10.0	—14.1	29.2	17.1
Harrison	73.4	33.5	30.3	16.0
Jackson	52.1	53.6	35.2	21.5
Pearl River	7.8	8.2	26.8	21.8
Stone	7.4	—14.3	n. o.	21.8
Old Cotton-Tobacco				
Adams	56.2	— 4.7	78.6	49.9
Amite	—14.6	— 9.7	59.4	54.2
Bolivar	10.1	—12.9	88.1	68.5
Carroll	—24.6	—25.2	58.4	57.0
Chickasaw	— 7.8	—15.9	59.0	44.5
Claiborne	—11.8	— 5.0	78.0	74.8
Clarke	— 6.8	— 4.8	47.9	40.7
Clay	2.2	—12.5	69.7	56.9
Coahoma	24.7	— 4.5	88.2	72.2
Copiah	—11.8	— 8.9	52.4	53.4
Covington	— 7.8	— 1.4	35.2	32.5
DeSoto	12.0	—15.1	74.8	67.2
Forrest	33.9	18.5	n. o.	28.8
Franklin	—11.9	—13.6	49.7	39.4
Grenada	13.4	—11.6	72.9	52.2

Hinds	51.0	15.3	75.2	45.0
Holmes	— 4.2	—19.8	77.9	73.5
Humphreys	0.8	—16.6	n. o.	69.7
Issaquena	31.7	—35.7	94.0	67.4
Jasper	— 7.6	1.9	48.6	51.4
Jefferson	—10.0	—21.9	81.1	74.5
Jefferson Davis	— 2.8	— 2.0	n. o.	55.5
Jones	20.4	6.1	26.2	26.3
Lafayette	16.0	— 5.7	44.0	35.5
Lamar	11.1	0.8	n. o.	15.9
Lawrence	—10.1	— 8.9	50.1	37.6
Lee	3.6	—12.8	39.4	27.9
Leflore	14.5	— 9.4	88.2	68.2
Lincoln	4.9	— 5.1	42.7	32.9
Lowndes	24.9	— 6.5	75.5	48.6
Madison	1.6	—13.2	79.8	73.6
Marion	2.7	— 6.0	32.0	35.0
Marshall	— 2.4	— 1.3	67.6	70.6
Monroe	6.0	—14.9	59.8	37.5
Noxubee	— 9.3	—25.6	84.8	74.4
Oktibbeha	41.4	—10.2	68.5	47.8
Panola	— 0.7	—14.9	66.7	55.9
Perry	0.4	— 8.8	32.8	24.3
Pike	0.7	0.0	49.8	44.7
Quitman	11.7	—13.1	76.9	60.7
Rankin	14.7	— 6.8	58.5	47.3
Sharkey	—14.1	—17.3	88.1	71.3
Simpson	— 2.6	2.6	38.7	33.3
Smith	—15.1	— 7.9	18.1	20.3
Sunflower	2.3	—12.4	75.0	68.1
Tallahatchie	— 5.1	—13.7	67.8	63.7
Tate	— 1.3	—10.4	59.1	57.6
Tunica	20.6	— 8.4	90.5	81.8
Walthall	—10.4	—12.2	n. o.	46.0
Warren	12.8	— 9.9	74.7	50.7
Washington	26.2	— 4.0	89.7	66.8
Wayne	— 3.3	7.7	40.3	36.6
Wilkinson	— 3.4	—14.7	79.6	69.1
Yalobusha	—13.6	—21.8	53.0	43.9
Yazoo	— 1.5	—15.9	77.1	61.8
Uplands				
Alcorn	4.5	—17.4	25.5	14.4
Attala	—10.5	—13.5	47.1	43.4
Benton	—16.5	—14.6	49.5	43.8
Calhoun	—13.7	— 6.2	24.8	23.3
Choctaw	—20.5	—14.5	27.5	30.2
Itawamba	—13.7	—11.0	9.9	5.4
Kemper	—25.5	—28.5	56.8	59.4

	Per Cent Change 1940 to 1950		Non-white as Per Cent of Total	
	White	Non-White	1900	1950
MISSISSIPPI (*Cont.*)				
Lauderdale	15.1	2.5	49.7	36.4
Leake	—14.6	— 8.4	35.9	42.4
Montgomery	— 7.8	— 7.9	51.8	43.0
Neshoba	— 8.7	— 4.8	17.9	25.9
Newton	— 4.6	— 9.9	38.6	34.6
Pontotoc	—11.3	—18.4	26.4	19.1
Prentiss	— 5.7	— 2.8	19.8	11.8
Scott	— 7.1	— 5.3	42.4	43.2
Tipah	—13.0	— 1.3	22.4	19.4
Tishomingo	— 7.6	—21.4	10.4	5.2
Union	— 5.5	—15.1	25.1	17.9
Webster	—16.0	—24.1	28.8	23.2
Winston	— 5.1	2.0	41.8	41.8
NORTH CAROLINA				
Coastal				
Brunswick	7.8	21.3	39.9	36.6
Camden	0.2	— 9.9	40.0	38.7
Carteret	29.3	7.6	18.0	12.6
Currituck	— 3.5	—15.2	27.2	32.0
Dare	— 9.8	—19.3	12.1	7.0
Hyde	—18.9	—15.7	43.3	42.2
New Hanover	40.7	16.2	50.8	31.4
Tyrrell	—16.5	3.9	29.4	41.4
Old Cotton-Tobacco				
Anson	— 5.1	— 6.6	53.4	48.6
Beaufort	2.8	0.5	42.9	37.3
Bertie	— 6.2	6.3	57.6	59.8
Bladen	9.3	9.4	46.5	41.2
Chatham	2.6	2.9	34.9	32.1
Chowan	15.2	0.6	57.0	43.6
Columbus	7.9	17.0	30.4	33.9
Craven	91.1	12.8	60.2	32.4
Cumberland	77.8	31.5	43.0	28.0
Duplin	1.2	7.2	38.1	37.0
Edgecombe	10.3	0.6	62.4	51.9
Franklin	— 1.7	9.6	49.5	45.6
Gates	—10.9	1.0	46.1	52.6
Greene	— 7.9	3.8	48.0	46.5
Halifax	3.8	3.0	64.1	56.6

Harnett	9.7	2.0	31.6	26.3
Hertford	8.7	12.4	58.7	60.0
Hoke	8.0	3.9	n. o.	60.6
Johnston	2.5	6.3	25.3	21.7
Jones	— 1.9	4.0	45.7	45.4
Lee	29.9	14.4	n. o.	26.0
Lenoir	11.7	11.6	43.2	43.1
Martin	3.2	11.0	47.6	50.4
Montgomery	6.1	5.6	25.9	22.9
Moore	12.1	— 4.8	33.2	26.9
Nash	6.9	8.9	41.7	42.4
Northampton	— 5.4	4.1	57.3	64.2
Onslow	170.4	37.4	30.2	15.9
Pamlico	3.3	2.3	32.8	34.6
Pasquotank	27.5	6.1	51.4	38.2
Pender	0.3	8.3	51.6	48.3
Perquimans	— 0.6	— 3.0	49.6	47.8
Pitt	6.6	1.5	50.2	46.3
Richmond	12.1	— 1.6	49.0	30.5
Robeson	8.2	19.1	41.9	57.3
Sampson	3.3	7.8	34.6	36.8
Scotland	27.3	1.2	53.5	47.8
Vance	9.3	4.6	58.5	45.5
Wake	32.6	8.7	44.6	29.3
Warren	— 1.7	3.5	68.2	66.4
Washington	8.3	5.3	50.6	43.6
Wayne	12.5	7.2	42.8	42.2
Wilson	11.4	4.6	42.0	40.4

Uplands

Alamance	23.9	24.4	26.2	18.5
Alexander	8.0	10.1	7.8	7.1
Burke	18.8	7.3	15.1	7.5
Cabarrus	8.9	— 0.4	27.2	15.3
Caldwell	21.9	11.9	12.3	6.9
Caswell	0.2	8.9	54.6	47.6
Catawba	20.9	8.4	13.5	9.1
Cleveland	11.2	9.5	19.2	21.9
Davidson	17.6	8.5	13.6	10.3
Davie	4.2	— 1.2	21.7	14.0
Durham	31.2	18.5	37.2	33.3
Forsyth	22.7	0.7	29.9	28.4
Gaston	28.0	18.2	26.0	13.4
Granville	17.9	— 0.8	51.1	46.7
Guilford	26.3	16.0	28.4	19.5
Iredell	13.4	4.4	25.2	17.8
Lincoln	17.6	5.6	19.1	12.7
Mecklenburg	35.5	23.0	43.2	25.4
Orange	62.0	20.9	35.8	25.1

	Per Cent Change 1940 to 1950		Non-white as Per Cent of Total	
	White	Non-White	1900	1950
NORTH CAROLINA (*Cont.*)				
Person	— 1.0	— 5.6	42.1	36.2
Polk	— 1.1	— 8.2	17.2	13.0
Randolph	15.6	— 0.5	13.0	8.5
Rockingham	13.0	7.9	35.0	20.1
Rowan	11.2	— 0.8	26.1	17.1
Rutherford	3.1	— 7.4	17.7	12.3
Stanley	13.8	8.0	11.8	11.4
Stokes	— 3.8	—15.7	15.1	9.0
Surry	9.5	3.0	11.4	5.7
Union	8.8	3.3	29.5	22.6
Wilkes	5.8	— 3.7	9.1	6.0
Yadkin	8.0	— 6.6	8.4	5.0
Highlands				
Alleghany	— 1.8	—13.3	6.0	3.3
Ashe	— 2.7	41.3	3.5	1.3
Avery	— 1.2	—21.2	n. o.	1.5
Buncombe	17.8	— 5.5	18.3	12.3
Cherokee	— 3.4	49.8	3.6	1.7
Clay	— 6.1	——	3.0	1.1
Graham	6.7	27.0	0.6	3.2
Haywood	8.5	— 7.2	3.8	2.2
Henderson	20.6	3.0	12.5	6.7
Jackson	— 0.9	4.4	5.0	7.6
McDowell	14.7	—21.3	15.1	5.6
Macon	2.6	—22.5	5.6	2.2
Malison	— 8.8	—13.1	2.7	0.9
Mitchell	— 5.2	——	3.5	0.3
Swain	—21.2	0.0	2.1	15.6
Transylvania	26.7	—10.6	9.3	4.9
Watauga	2.1	—37.4	2.9	1.2
Yancey	— 5.4	17.1	2.5	1.1
OKLAHOMA [1]				
Uplands				
Alfalfa	—24.3	——		——
Beaver	—14.3	——	0.6	——
Beckham	— 2.7	13.4		1.9
Blaine	—19.4	—28.1	10.4	12.9
Bryan	—22.7	—48.3		6.4
Caddo	—17.8	—17.1		12.0

Canadian	— 7.4	0.0	2.3	7.5
Carter	—14.2	—25.2		11.0
Choctaw	—28.0	—27.6		22.0
Cimarron	25.2	—		0.3
Cleveland	50.1	—24.7	2.9	1.2
Comanche	36.7	135.2		11.1
Cotton	—22.1	38.8		5.2
Creek	—20.5	—40.5		11.1
Custer	—10.4	39.0	1.5	6.4
Dewey	—27.2	—	0.8	3.1
Ellis	—13.5	—		—
Garfield	15.6	28.4	1.7	3.0
Garvin	— 3.4	—31.6		4.3
Grady	—15.3	—12.9		5.4
Grant	—20.4	—	0.5	0.1
Greer	—19.7	— 6.8	0.1	4.3
Harmon	—20.8	44.4		3.9
Harper	— 7.4	—		—
Hughes	—29.5	38.5		13.0
Jackson	—11.9	— 6.9		6.2
Jefferson	—26.2	—25.7		1.9
Johnston	—33.9	—33.7		8.3
Kay	4.1	— 7.9	1.2	4.4
Kingfisher	—14.8	—42.5	13.3	9.1
Kiowa	—16.7	—27.0		7.1
Lincoln	—24.0	37.6	8.0	8.2
Logan	—13.4	— 7.8	23.0	22.5
Love	—32.8	— 8.6		6.9
McClain	—24.2	—18.3		4.1
Major	—13.9	—		0.2
Marshall	—33.6	—30.6		6.6
Murray	—22.0	—24.6		4.8
Noble	—16.9	—35.9	3.2	6.3
Nowata	—15.0	—31.3		8.1
Okfuskee	—35.8	—39.6		29.3
Oklahoma	34.6	14.1	11.4	8.6
Okmulgee	— 5.4	—33.6		19.6
Osage	—18.5	—19.6		6.5
Ottawa	— 9.4	—		3.2
Pawnee	—21.8	—34.4	1.6	8.9
Payne	31.2	—25.1	2.2	3.2
Pontotoc	—22.9	—22.2		5.4
Pottawatomie	—20.1	—29.5	3.1	6.0
Roger Mills	—31.9	—	—	2.0
Rogers	— 6.6	—21.2		5.6
Seminole	—33.6	—45.8		15.3
Stephens	9.1	57.0		2.2
Texas	43.6	—		0.2
Tillman	—15.0	—17.4		11.5

	Per Cent Change 1940 to 1950		Non-white as Per Cent of Total	
	White	Non-White	1900	1950
OKLAHOMA (*Cont.*)				
Tulsa	31.6	16.8		9.1
Washington	9.8	— 4.1		5.1
Washita	—20.7	——	——	1.4
Woods	— 2.7	——	0.5	——
Woodward	—11.7	——	0.1	0.2
Highlands				
Adair	3.3	——		17.1
Atoka	—24.5	—15.9		9.6
Cherokee	— 7.1	—50.5		18.2
Coal	—37.0	—49.2		7.1
Craig	—10.6	—20.4		5.2
Delaware	—20.9	——		15.9
Haskell	—21.7	—37.6		4.1
Latimer	—24.8	—29.4		10.5
LeFlore	—23.7	—30.4		7.4
McCurtain	—23.4	—28.7		24.9
McIntosh	—26.3	—28.5		23.4
Mayes	— 7.7	—57.0		7.7
Muskogee	3.2	—11.1		23.0
Pittsburg	—15.2	—13.8		10.0
Pushmataha	—37.8	—43.8		7.8
Sequoyah	—11.4	—36.7		10.7
Wagoner	—20.9	—29.0		24.6
SOUTH CAROLINA				
Coastal				
Beaufort	58.1	5.0	90.5	57.5
Charleston	56.9	14.7	68.5	41.5
Georgetown	35.8	9.7	76.6	53.1
Old Cotton-Tobacco				
Aiken	16.3	— 7.7	55.4	36.4
Allendale	—11.0	9.5	n. o.	72.3
Bamberg	0.8	10.3	67.3	57.8
Barnwell	—12.0	15.6	71.6	61.7
Berkeley	16.7	8.7	78.7	63.2
Calhoun	— 1.1	—12.0	n. o.	70.8
Chester	11.1	—11.9	67.7	42.2
Chesterfield	— 0.7	3.2	39.9	39.0
Clarendon	5.1	1.1	71.5	70.9

Colleton	7.7	7.3	66.6	53.3
Darlington	18.5	2.9	59.6	46.4
Dillon	7.4	1.4	n. o.	48.3
Dorchester	19.3	9.1	61.9	55.2
Edgefield	1.0	—12.1	71.2	59.9
Fairfield	— 3.9	—13.7	76.0	59.3
Florence	13.7	12.0	58.5	44.9
Greenwood	15.2	—15.5	66.7	30.2
Hampton	7.8	— 0.1	65.3	55.9
Horry	15.5	14.3	27.1	26.9
Jasper	— 3.3	1.6	n. o.	65.2
Kershaw	8.1	—10.6	59.5	48.8
Lancaster	19.0	— 5.9	49.8	28.9
Lee	—10.8	— 5.0	n. o.	66.9
Lexington	28.6	6.0	37.8	21.4
McCormick	7.5	—14.8	n. o.	62.6
Marion	9.7	10.2	51.6	56.0
Marlboro	— 0.3	— 8.1	59.4	52.7
Newberry	3.2	—17.0	65.7	37.2
Orangeburg	6.3	8.8	69.5	63.2
Richland	47.4	19.2	61.6	35.4
Saluda	— 4.3	—11.2	53.5	42.6
Sumter	31.7	— 2.2	74.9	57.3
Williamsburg	3.2	8.7	62.7	67.6

Uplands

Abbeville	13.2	—22.8	66.1	33.5
Anderson	9.2	17.5	42.2	21.3
Cherokee	6.9	— 0.6	34.6	22.1
Greenville	28.7	3.6	36.4	18.7
Laurens	16.3	—10.6	59.3	31.1
Oconee	11.5	—17.2	25.8	12.2
Pickens	10.5	— 8.6	24.8	11.2
Spartanburg	20.0	10.4	32.3	22.4
Union	5.8	—10.6	57.1	32.1
York	32.6	3.7	52.4	31.0

TENNESSEE

Old Cotton-Tobacco

Carroll	5.3	—14.5	23.0	13.2
Chester	4.1	—20.0	20.5	12.9
Crockett	— 5.2	0.1	25.5	21.7
Dyer	— 3.2	— 9.7	24.2	13.8
Fayette	— 3.0	—11.5	73.0	70.6
Gibson	6.7	9.7	26.2	21.0
Hardeman	— 1.3	— 1.0	44.4	37.4
Hayward	— 1.4	— 7.6	67.8	61.9
Lake	13.2	—19.7	26.9	22.2
Lauderdale	6.4	— 4.3	46.3	34.8

	Per Cent Change 1940 to 1950		Non-white as Per Cent of Total	
	White	Non-White	1900	1950
TENNESSEE (*Cont.*)				
Madison	16.0	2.5	46.1	33.2
Obion	— 4.0	—20.5	17.1	11.2
Shelby	48.9	16.0	55.2	37.4
Tipton	10.9	— 1.0	47.7	36.5
Uplands				
Bedford	5.4	—16.8	26.3	12.6
Benton	— 4.2	2.8	4.5	2.5
Bradley	15.3	—11.2	13.2	5.5
Cheatham	— 6.7	—17.8	16.4	8.0
Clay	—20.4	—13.3	4.4	2.8
Davidson	28.4	13.5	35.7	20.0
Decatur	— 7.8	—11.4	11.7	6.0
DeKalb	19.5	—32.8	6.7	2.6
Dickson	— 3.2	—18.6	15.7	7.7
Giles	— 4.4	—18.6	34.5	21.0
Granger	— 8.6	—20.2	4.2	1.6
Greene	4.6	— 9.7	5.1	2.8
Hamblen	30.2	14.5	14.1	7.7
Hamilton	17.6	7.4	31.6	20.4
Hardin	— 3.8	—18.7	13.9	7.3
Hawkins	6.9	6.1	8.9	3.5
Henderson	—11.7	0.4	14.6	9.9
Henry	— 6.4	—15.5	24.8	15.4
Hickman	— 9.6	—18.3	16.0	6.0
Houston	—16.8	—23.9	16.3	6.8
Humphries	—10.9	—16.1	11.3	5.3
Jackson	—17.7	—50.0	3.1	0.9
Jefferson	6.5	—10.2	11.7	5.0
Knox	27.4	18.1	15.9	9.6
Lawrence	0.8	—19.3	6.3	2.0
Lewis	6.2	—43.9	8.8	2.4
Lincoln	— 4.6	—12.5	23.1	14.2
Loudon	17.8	—12.5	12.5	2.3
McMinn	5.2	—13.7	10.4	4.9
McNairy	0.0	— 3.0	13.8	6.4
Macon	— 8.7	—15.4	6.8	1.4
Marshall	12.5	0.1	22.7	11.8
Maury	5.2	—15.3	42.5	21.3
Meigs	— 4.3	—16.0	8.9	4.8
Montgomery	46.3	— 0.3	44.9	22.2

Perry	—14.3	—13.5	7.6	3.2
Rhea	— 1.0	—17.6	13.1	4.4
Roane	14.2	8.4	11.5	4.8
Robertson	— 4.9	—15.5	27.3	17.9
Rutherford	26.8	— 1.6	38.7	16.4
Smith	—11.5	—30.1	15.8	5.1
Stewart	—31.8	—44.0	15.4	3.0
Sullivan	38.6	5.8	6.3	2.4
Sumner	4.4	—10.0	25.6	11.8
Trousdale	— 9.0	—12.8	33.9	17.9
Washington	17.6	— 6.8	9.5	4.8
Wayne	2.6	—31.2	8.8	2.0
Weakley	— 4.0	—16.3	13.0	7.3
Williamson	— 2.1	— 8.9	36.6	21.1
Wilson	7.6	—11.3	26.8	15.4

Highlands

Anderson	121.5	264.8	6.3	3.1
Bledsoe	4.1	—20.2	7.2	5.3
Blount	32.9	35.9	8.4	5.2
Campbell	10.8	—16.6	3.6	1.2
Cannon	— 7.1	— 8.8	6.8	3.1
Carter	21.4	—19.1	4.0	1.0
Claiborne	1.2	—31.1	3.5	1.4
Cocke	— 4.5	— 4.2	6.6	2.8
Coffee	23.3	— 6.2	11.6	4.4
Cumberland	21.0	—	6.9	0.1
Fentress	4.6	—	0.4	—
Franklin	8.3	— 8.6	16.9	9.3
Grundy	9.0	—	4.0	0.3
Hancock	—18.1	—52.6	2.4	1.2
Johnson	— 5.5	— 7.8	3.5	1.4
Marion	8.0	— 3.0	12.2	6.7
Monroe	1.5	—11.4	6.6	3.3
Moore	— 5.7	29.5	8.2	8.2
Morgan	3.7	—17.2	6.3	2.2
Overton	— 6.9	—	2.0	0.5
Pickett	—18.0	—	0.2	—
Polk	— 9.1	—	2.7	0.6
Putnam	14.1	— 1.4	4.5	1.9
Scott	8.7	—	3.0	0.1
Sequatchie	12.7	—	1.1	0.1
Sevier	0.4	— 1.4	2.6	0.9
Unicoi	12.4	—	2.2	0.1
Union	— 4.0	—	0.6	—
Van Buren	— 1.2	—	1.8	0.6
Warren	14.0	— 5.8	12.6	5.6
White	2.4	—22.8	7.2	3.1

	Per Cent Change 1940 to 1950		Non-white as Per Cent of Total	
	White	Non-White	1900	1950
TEXAS				
Coastal				
Aransas	21.8	—	11.0	2.5
Brazoria	99.2	— 4.0	55.3	14.7
Calhoun	59.5	24.2	11.3	7.7
Cameron	50.9	4.4	1.1	0.8
Chambers	9.5	—10.7	27.2	19.7
Galveston	40.8	33.9	19.9	21.1
Harris	54.5	44.5	31.2	18.7
Jackson	12.7	— 3.8	35.9	13.3
Jefferson	35.4	30.5	27.7	22.7
Kenedy	— 9.7	—	n. o.	—
Kleberg	65.4	50.9	n. o.	3.7
Matagorda	10.7	— 2.7	62.2	7.4
Nueces	80.4	49.1	5.5	4.9
Orange	136.1	113.2	17.2	10.9
Refugio	— 3.1	1.8	28.1	11.1
San Patricio	24.9	— 4.1	1.5	2.0
Victoria	36.6	— 1.4	27.7	9.9
Willacy	59.2	—26.7	n. o.	0.6
Old Cotton-Tobacco				
Anderson	—13.0	—16.3	41.5	31.0
Bastrop	— 7.5	—12.7	38.6	31.6
Bowie	33.7	— 0.2	38.2	24.6
Brazos	72.2	— 8.2	46.9	24.0
Burleson	—23.9	—37.9	45.3	32.3
Camp	—13.3	—17.5	47.6	39.8
Cass	—18.7	—23.1	39.0	32.4
Cherokee	—10.7	—15.3	32.6	27.5
Colorado	6.4	—18.7	43.4	25.2
Free Stone	—25.1	—26.7	43.9	40.3
Gregg	6.2	3.8	55.9	24.5
Grimes	—31.4	—30.6	54.9	40.4
Harrison	8.0	—16.4	68.1	51.8
Houston	—27.8	—25.0	40.6	39.1
Jasper	18.4	5.2	42.0	26.5
Lee	—18.1	—26.3	29.8	26.6
Leon	—28.7	—37.0	38.4	39.4
Liberty	11.8	0.0	29.2	22.7
Madison	—34.2	—32.1	23.6	32.8
Marion	— 7.4	—13.9	66.5	9.6

Montgomery	15.4	—13.9	38.8	7.8
Morris	3.5	—15.9	40.7	8.9
Nacogdoches	—16.3	— 8.9	27.1	8.6
Newton	—13.9	—31.3	34.1	8.4
Panola	— 1.5	—31.6	43.0	34.6
Polk	—20.0	—25.2	33.6	29.6
Red River	—27.6	—23.1	28.2	23.9
Robertson	—21.8	—23.6	53.2	41.3
Rusk	—15.8	—19.7	42.3	29.8
Sabine	—24.6	—10.8	27.4	26.1
San Augustine	—34.9	—14.9	34.6	34.7
San Jacinto	—21.1	—20.5	53.8	52.5
Shelby	—19.5	—20.4	20.1	25.5
Smith	11.9	0.2	42.9	29.9
Upshur	—21.4	—18.1	30.5	28.9
Walker	14.6	—15.0	52.6	37.2
Waller	6.5	26.7	55.3	52.9
Washington	—13.9	—27.6	48.7	34.1
Wharton	4.8	—14.8	51.5	21.8

Uplands

Andrews	290.9	——	——	0.8
Angelina	10.0	22.5	16.0	16.5
Archer	—10.4	——	0.1	0.3
Armstrong	—11.4	——	0.2	0.5
Atascosa	3.8	24.7	3.9	1.2
Austin	—10.3	—31.4	30.0	20.6
Bailey	19.2	61.1	n. o.	3.2
Bandera	3.9	——	1.7	0.4
Baylor	—11.2	—21.7	0.5	1.6
Bee	10.9	— 8.9	6.2	2.6
Bell	64.0	68.7	8.4	12.0
Bexar	47.6	53.5	12.3	6.7
Blanco	—10.5	—32.5	4.8	2.8
Bordon	—21.3	——	0.3	2.3
Bosque	—24.9	—25.9	4.9	3.2
Brewster	13.5	——	3.4	0.5
Briscoe	—13.4	——	——	2.8
Brooks	44.8	——	n. o.	0.4
Brown	9.2	60.1	1.3	3.2
Burnet	— 4.3	20.8	2.5	2.1
Caldwell	—22.5	—21.0	26.1	15.9
Callahan	—21.4	——	0.3	0.1
Carson	3.5	——	0.4	0.2
Castro	15.6	——	n. o.	1.2
Childress	— 3.7	93.1	——	6.9
Clay	—20.8	——	0.5	0.9
Cochran	57.4	——	——	2.8
Coke	—11.2	——	0.1	0.1

	Per Cent Change 1940 to 1950		Non-white as Per Cent of Total	
	White	Non-White	1900	1950
TEXAS (Cont.)				
Coleman	—25.1	— 1.2	0.9	2.6
Collin	—12.4	— 3.7	4.9	9.2
Collingsworth	—14.9	75.4	0.2	7.4
Comal	33.7	— 3.7	3.7	1.7
Comanche	—19.4	——	——	0.1
Concho	—17.8	——	1.0	0.2
Cooke	—11.4	— 2.8	6.8	4.4
Coryell	—19.0	—34.6	2.7	2.6
Cottle	—14.5	— 2.3	——	6.4
Crane	37.4	——	——	2.6
Crockett	43.8	— 7.0	0.5	2.7
Crosby	— 5.9	10.5	0.4	8.7
Culberson	10.8	——	n. o.	0.3
Dallam	17.1	——	——	0.5
Dallas	57.8	35.1	16.5	13.6
Dawson	21.2	119.4	——	5.7
Deaf Smith	50.4	——	0.1	0.1
Delta	—31.7	—14.5	6.3	10.4
Denton	24.0	6.6	7.3	5.7
DeWitt	— 6.4	—15.9	23.2	14.0
Dickens	— 9.2	5.7	——	5.5
Dimmit	24.3	——	3.7	0.6
Donley	—17.8	7.2	1.8	4.1
Duval	—23.6	——	0.1	0.2
Eastland	—20.8	—37.5	0.3	1.4
Ector	178.9	203.2	0.8	3.8
Edwards	— 0.9	——	0.4	0.4
Ellis	— 6.0	1.5	2.5	23.8
El Paso	—48.6	56.8	9.7	2.4
Erath	—11.0	—32.2	1.9	0.9
Falls	—24.3	—28.6	35.9	32.2
Fannin	—24.0	—23.3	10.6	10.6
Fayette	—11.7	—37.7	28.4	16.3
Fisher	—15.6	5.0	0.1	5.1
Floyd	— 2.4	49.2	0.4	3.7
Foard	—24.5	91.2	——	10.3
Fort Bend	— 1.3	—17.5	65.4	24.2
Franklin	—25.7	—19.2	10.7	6.8
Frio	12.8	—10.0	3.9	1.0
Gaines	9.8	9.8	——	1.3

Garza	9.2	61.6	1.1	3.9
Gillespie	— 1.1	——	1.3	0.1
Glasscock	— 8.0	——	0.3	1.0
Goliad	—29.4	—28.9	21.7	10.3
Gonzales	—16.2	—28.7	29.9	18.6
Gray	2.2	84.4	2.7	2.7
Grayson	3.2	— 8.8	12.2	8.8
Guadalupe	1.4	—12.4	24.3	14.3
Hale	47.7	145.5	0.2	3.8
Hall	—15.1	141.6	——	9.0
Hamilton	—19.9	——	0.1	0.1
Hansford	50.8	——	0.6	0.1
Hardeman	—10.5	42.2	0.5	8.0
Hardin	24.1	17.6	18.8	15.8
Hartley	1.7	——	0.3	0.6
Haskell	—10.6	61.3	0.2	6.6
Hays	20.1	—19.0	15.1	6.4
Hemphill	— 1.1	——	0.2	——
Henderson	—27.5	—22.0	21.8	20.4
Hidalgo	50.9	103.3	1.6	0.9
Hill	—20.4	— 8.0	7.2	15.0
Hockley	58.1	146.0	——	4.6
Hood	—20.3	——	2.6	0.6
Hopkins	—23.4	—13.4	13.6	11.2
Howard	26.6	49.7	3.4	3.3
Hudspeth	41.6	—79.7	n. o.	0.6
Hunt	—14.3	0.4	9.2	14.8
Hutchinson	65.0	116.2	——	1.8
Irion	—18.8	——	0.5	0.9
Jack	—24.1	——	1.1	1.0
Jeff Davis	—12.4	——	3.7	1.3
Jim Hogg	— 0.6	——	n. o.	0.3
Jim Wells	38.8	12.1	n. o.	1.5
Johnson	2.3	13.6	3.4	5.6
Jones	— 6.8	28.4	0.1	6.0
Karnes	— 9.9	—31.2	7.3	3.9
Kaufman	—19.9	—15.3	18.3	28.6
Kendall	7.1	——	5.7	1.2
Kent	—34.1	——	——	2.1
Kerr	22.4	—13.2	3.0	4.1
Kimble	— 8.5	——	0.2	0.1
King	—23.0	——	——	7.1
Kinney	—42.7	—15.5	14.3	8.4
Knox	— 3.2	95.5	——	6.1
Lamar	—15.0	—13.2	22.6	18.6
Lamb	10.7	84.5	——	6.6
Lampasas	9.2	—21.7	4.3	2.0
La Salle	— 6.6	——	2.7	0.2

| | Per Cent Change 1940 to 1950 | | Non-white as Per cent of Total | |
	White	Non-White	1900	1950
TEXAS (Cont.)				
Lavaca	—10.7	—29.2	17.4	10.3
Limestone	—26.1	—23.2	19.5	29.8
Lipscomb	— 5.5	——	——	0.1
Live Oak	— 7.5	——	3.2	0.4
Llano	—10.5	——	0.5	1.0
Loving	—20.7	——	——	0.4
Lubbock	91.2	158.1	——	7.9
Lynn	— 8.5	13.1	——	5.4
McCulloch	—11.0	—21.4	0.8	3.2
McLennan	30.9	14.7	24.1	17.2
McMullen	—13.9	——	3.2	0.4
Martin	— 2.7	102.3	0.6	5.1
Mason	— 7.5	——	1.0	11.1
Maverick	21.9	——	4.8	4.8
Medina	6.2	—26.0	4.6	8.0
Menard	— 7.3	——	1.0	10.3
Midland	120.2	117.8	3.2	2.9
Milam	27.5	—33.0	26.4	11.5
Mills	—24.6	——	0.2	12.7
Mitchell	15.2	13.4	4.9	6.1
Montague	—16.5	——	0.1	10.9
Moore	199.1	——	——	1.6
Motley	—21.7	— 2.6	——	8.3
Navarro	—22.2	—22.3	20.9	10.6
Nolan	14.4	15.1	0.8	4.0
Ochiltree	42.8	——	——	0.1
Oldham	21.0	——	0.3	0.1
Palo Pinto	— 8.0	22.6	2.4	3.9
Parker	5.2	0.8	3.3	1.2
Parmer	— 1.5	——	n. o.	0.3
Pecos	21.0	70.0	0.9	1.4
Potter	35.4	31.9	0.8	4.9
Presidio	—33.2	——	1.4	1.0
Rains	—42.6	—33.4	8.8	10.0
Randall	92.3	——	0.1	0.4
Reagan	52.8	227.9	n. o.	4.5
Real	2.1	——	n. o.	0.3
Reeves	48.3	1.1	0.6	2.4
Roberts	—20.6	——	1.5	——
Rockwall	—14.4	— 7.9	4.7	27.5
Runnels	—11.5	2.8	0.6	3.1

San Saba	—20.8	—56.9	0.8	0.8
Schleicher	— 7.1	—16.8	2.5	3.5
Scurry	97.8	68.6	——	1.5
Shackelford	—19.2	—29.2	5.4	2.8
Sherman	20.5	——	2.9	0.1
Somervell	—17.3	——	0.2	0.1
Starr	4.7	——	1.2	0.1
Stephens	—14.8	5.0	0.1	3.4
Sterling	— 8.1	——	0.2	1.0
Stonewall	—32.9	—60.3	——	2.8
Sutton	— 4.7	——	0.3	0.9
Swisher	25.6	——	——	1.3
Tarrant	63.2	39.7	11.0	11.0
Taylor	43.0	56.9	1.7	4.1
Terrell	8.7	——	n. o.	0.4
Terry	17.3	22.3	——	2.9
Throckmorton	—15.4	——	0.1	——
Titus	—12.5	2.9	17.5	18.5
Tom Green	50.4	42.4	13.2	5.1
Travis	51.2	15.6	28.1	14.1
Trinity	—31.0	—12.1	25.6	26.8
Tyler	— 7.0	1.2	20.1	19.8
Upton	24.8	— 1.9	——	3.9
Uvalde	21.4	— 7.1	2.8	1.2
Val Verde	7.4	19.7	3.0	2.2
Van Zandt	—27.3	—29.6	5.4	6.9
Ward	36.6	— 1.4	0.2	2.4
Webb	22.5	—33.0	0.9	0.2
Wheeler	—17.9	47.0	2.2	2.9
Wichita	33.3	41.5	3.5	6.4
Wilbarger	— 0.1	5.2	0.7	8.6
Williamson	— 5.5	—13.9	11.4	15.1
Wilson	—13.8	—23.5	8.0	2.2
Winkler	64.8	26.6	——	1.8
Wise	—15.2	—28.6	0.6	0.9
Wood	—11.8	—16.4	19.1	14.7
Yoakum	—17.4	——	——	0.3
Young	—11.2	—39.0	0.1	0.9
Zapata	12.5	——	——	——
Zavala	— 3.8	——	0.1	0.9

VIRGINIA

Coastal

Accomack	8.8	— 8.0	36.3	34.2
Charles City	— 3.2	12.8	73.3	81.0
Elizabeth City	73.1	60.8	44.1	20.5
Essex	3.9	—16.8	63.1	46.1
Gloucester	11.5	1.9	51.5	31.3

	Per Cent Change 1940 to 1950		Non-white as Per cent of Total	
	White	Non-White	1900	1950
VIRGINIA (*Cont.*)				
Isle of Wight	10.5	12.3	47.8	51.9
James City	23.3	35.5	52.7	46.5
King and Queen	—10.9	— 8.2	56.8	53.8
King William	2.5	— 9.4	59.2	46.1
Lancaster	1.7	— 6.1	54.7	41.2
Mathews	— 0.2	0.6	29.1	24.9
Middlesex	3.2	— 2.7	55.2	41.9
Nansemond	17.1	7.8	56.2	65.3
New Kent	7.1	— 9.2	65.9	54.0
Norfolk	257.7	31.1	62.2	16.3
Northampton	— 0.7	— 2.6	55.4	53.5
Northumberland	— 3.5	— 5.5	42.3	40.8
Princess Anne	164.4	28.2	25.8	23.5
Richmond	— 1.0	—16.0	41.3	34.4
Surry	— 6.0	4.5	61.2	63.8
Warwick	309.4	12.7	76.3	31.2
Westmoreland	10.3	2.6	52.6	45.5
York	54.0	— 4.6	54.5	26.2
Old Cotton-Tobacco				
Brunswick	— 2.3	7.0	59.5	57.8
Greensville	11.7	8.5	65.1	59.3
Lunenburg	2.7	1.0	56.1	43.9
Mecklenburg	8.4	1.5	61.0	49.5
Southampton	1.6	— 0.7	59.9	60.9
Sussex	6.6	0.3	65.9	65.6
Uplands				
Albemarle	14.9	—12.6	36.3	18.6
Amelia	— 5.2	— 8.6	66.2	49.9
Amherst	4.1	— 8.3	39.5	27.9
Appomattox	0.2	—11.1	40.7	24.7
Arlington [2]	147.7	32.3	38.4	4.9
Augusta	—18.0	—46.5	17.6	5.1
Bedford	2.8	—11.4	32.1	19.0
Botetourt	— 2.5	—17.7	22.6	10.1
Buckingham	— 9.1	— 7.2	51.4	42.8
Campbell	14.0	1.8	41.3	23.7
Caroline	—12.6	— 8.5	54.1	51.4
Charlotte	— 9.4	—14.1	55.7	40.9
Chesterfield	27.8	34.9	40.9	20.9

Clarke	0.1	— 6.9	28.1	17.2
Culpeper	4.3	—12.2	42.9	27.9
Cumberland	2.8	— 7.8	69.0	55.7
Dinwiddie	3.3	3.9	61.8	64.6
Fairfax	157.8	51.1	26.9	10.0
Faquier	5.1	— 8.9	35.5	26.3
Fluvanna	7.2	—10.0	44.3	35.1
Franklin	— 5.3	— 3.7	22.9	14.6
Frederick	26.2	— 6.3	5.7	2.2
Goochland	10.1	1.6	58.4	50.0
Greene	— 7.5	—18.2	23.0	13.5
Halifax	1.8	— 1.3	51.8	44.0
Hanover	27.4	3.2	44.8	30.8
Henrico	47.6	—18.5	42.6	9.9
Henry	22.6	5.3	43.5	24.2
King George	34.9	1.0	48.0	27.4
Loudoun	6.0	— 2.8	26.7	18.8
Louisa	— 4.9	— 8.0	52.2	39.8
Madison	0.9	—11.4	34.5	23.1
Montgomery	43.6	1.2	18.5	5.3
Nelson	—10.8	—11.8	35.3	27.0
Nottoway	3.4	— 5.1	59.8	43.9
Orange	3.8	— 6.6	43.9	26.7
Page	2.8	—16.0	10.4	3.7
Pittsylvania	6.9	7.5	45.4	30.9
Powhatan	— 0.9	— 3.4	65.7	43.6
Prince Edward	10.4	— 4.6	64.9	44.6
Prince George	87.8	21.1	62.7	30.3
Prince William	31.2	5.4	50.8	11.9
Pulaski	24.1	0.5	22.2	7.5
Rappahannock	—10.5	—31.9	30.8	17.7
Roanoke	— 4.0	5.4	24.3	8.5
Rockbridge	6.2	—11.7	18.7	8.6
Rockingham	13.0	—20.5	7.9	1.9
Shenendoah	1.1	15.4	3.2	1.8
Smyth	4.9	—10.1	6.8	1.6
Spotsylvania	27.5	2.1	42.1	23.9
Stafford	28.0	5.9	19.9	12.9
Warren	32.2	12.7	16.6	8.0
Washington	— 1.2	—15.2	8.8	3.2
Wythe	4.1	—19.8	13.6	4.7
Highlands				
Alleghany	3.1	— 8.6	24.6	8.3
Bath	—11.9	—16.9	18.0	10.5
Bland	— 4.7	11.2	3.9	2.0
Buchanan	13.6	—	0.1	—
Carroll	2.8	19.0	1.8	1.5
Craig	— 7.6	—	6.1	0.5

	Per Cent Change 1940 to 1950		Non-white as Per cent of Total	
	White	Non-White	1900	1950
VIRGINIA (*Cont.*)				
Dickenson	11.4	—41.5	—	1.4
Floyd	— 5.3	— 2.2	7.0	4.3
Giles	31.1	—11.7	7.4	2.5
Grayson	— 3.1	13.5	5.7	4.4
Highland	—17.5	37.2	6.7	2.9
Lee	— 7.7	—36.5	3.7	1.1
Patrick	— 6.0	— 4.2	10.5	8.4
Russel	0.9	— 4.5	4.2	2.5
Scott	2.6	—11.7	2.8	1.0
Tazewell	15.6	— 3.5	15.3	6.1
Wise	8.7	—16.2	10.0	4.2
Independent Cities [3]				
Alexandria (Arlington)	91.2	44.5	31.2	12.4
Bristol (Washington)	70.0	7.4	22.4	7.1
Buena Vista (Rockbridge)	22.6	—16.9	17.2	4.2
Charlottesville (Albemarle)	39.4	13.6	40.5	18.2
Clifton Forge (Alleghany)	— 8.9	—15.8	n. o.	18.1
Colonial Heights (Chesterfield)	n. o.	n. o.	n. o.	0.2
Danville (Pittsylvania)	8.4	4.1	39.4	30.2
Falls Church (Fairfax)	n. o.	n. o.	n. o.	1.8
Fredericksburg (Spotsylvania)	24.2	5.5	32.0	16.1
Hampton (Elizabeth City)	— 9.6	26.8	n. o.	37.2
Harrisonburg (Rockingham)	26.6	—11.7	n. o.	6.3
Hopewell (Prince George)	19.1	10.5	n. o.	14.8

Lynchburg (Campbell)	8.6	2.4	43.7	22.0
Martinsville (Henry)	51.2	150.8	n. o.	29.3
Newport News (Warwick)	10.5	19.6	34.6	43.2
Norfolk (Norfolk)	52.7	37.7	43.4	29.7
Petersburg (Dinwiddie)	18.2	9.7	49.3	42.2
Portsmouth (Norfolk)	57.7	57.8	32.3	38.4
Radford (Montgomery)	29.0	9.0	13.6	7.0
Richmond (Henrico)	19.4	19.2	37.9	31.7
Roanoke (Roanoke)	36.9	13.9	27.1	15.9
South Norfolk (Norfolk)	24.7	50.6	n. o.	23.0
Staunton (Augusta)	51.9	31.9	25.1	10.9
Suffolk (Nansemond)	4.1	17.9	n. o.	36.7
Waynesboro (Augusta)	n. o.	n. o.	n. o.	8.2
Williamsburg (James City, York)	88.7	4.6	n. o.	13.0
Winchester (Frederick)	15.1	7.9	21.4	8.3

SOURCES: 12th, 16th, and 17th Censuses of the United States.

1. Oklahoma, 1900, includes only counties in the territory of Oklahoma, but does not include Indian reservations within the Oklahoma Territory or the entire Indian Territory.

2. Previously Alexandria County.

3. Some changes in population of the independent cities may be due to the annexations and reversions occurring between censuses. In the case of recently incorporated independent cities, only data for 1950 is shown.

PART THREE

Appendices

Acknowledgment

The forty-five scholars who are listed later produced the research upon which this volume is based, and any list of acknowledgments must begin with recognition of my debt to them. It would be enormous if they had simply delivered on schedule the studies for which they were so precipitously retained; the fact is that most of them went far beyond that minimum call of duty.

There would have been no staff of scholars, of course, without the financing provided by the Fund for the Advancement of Education. But that benevolent organization did a great deal more than simply pick up the check. Alvin C. Eurich, the Fund's vice-president, gave the project its initial impetus, and often came to its rescue in its fledgling days. And Philip Coombs, the Fund's director of research, nursed it tenderly all along the way, with an able assist from his deputy, John Scanlon. The mark of their sound professional guidance is evident in whatever technical excellence this work may possess.

It was impossible for me to comply with the Fund's original suggestion—that I take leave from my duties as executive editor of the *Arkansas Gazette* and devote full time to the directorship of the project. The result was that the primary responsibility for assembling the temporary research staff, assigning specific functions, riding herd upon its diverse activities, and preparing a working digest of its findings fell upon Philip G. Hammer. On leave from his post as executive officer of the Committee of the South of the National Planning Association, Phil Hammer brought many necessary qualities to the task, but perhaps the most essential were boundless enthusiasm and inexhaustible energy.

In the final stages of preparation of this volume I have received indispensable assistance from Harold C. Fleming, assistant director of the Southern Regional Council. He has served as a knowledgeable ferret in running down essential facts in the great mass of research material and outside it, and his wit and perception have immeasurably lightened my task. I am also indebted to the other members of the Atlanta staff which was established to coordinate the research: Mozell Hill of Atlanta University, John A. Griffin of Emory University, and Ruth A. Morton of the American Friends Service Committee. The graphics were prepared by Miss Sara Love of New York.

I have consulted with a great many people in the course of the project and have received much sound advice. Few of these had an opportunity to consider the undertaking as a whole, and their listing here implies no responsibility on their part for its result—only my gratitude for their interest. The advice and counsel of Alexander Heard of the University of North Carolina helped set the project on course. George Mitchell of the Southern Regional Council gave me the benefit of his years of experience in the field of race relations. Curtis Dixon of the Southern Educational Foundation extended not only sound advice but warm hospitality to the Atlanta staff. Forrest Rozzel of the Arkansas Education Association helped establish essential contacts that might not otherwise have been available. And among the professional colleagues and old friends to whom I have turned at one time or another for aid and comfort are Ralph McGill of the Atlanta *Constitution,* Hodding Carter of the Greenville (Miss.) *Delta Democrat-Times,* C. A. McKnight of the Charlotte *News,* George Chaplin of the New Orleans *Item,* Grover Hall of the *Montgomery Advertiser,* and John Popham of the New York *Times.*

The manuscript benefited much from critical review by Howard W. Odum of the University of North Carolina, President Benjamin Mays of Morehouse College, Representative Brooks

Hays of Arkansas, Ira Reid of Haverford College, President Charles Johnson of Fisk University, Will Alexander of Chapel Hill, and the members of the Board of Directors of the Fund. Finally, I owe a considerable personal debt to J. N. Heiskell, the president and editor of the *Arkansas Gazette,* and Hugh B. Patterson, Jr., its publisher, who have been tolerant of my frequent absences and generally abstracted air during recent months; to Mary Powell, my secretary; and to my wife and daughter, who must have wondered what ever became of me.

H. S. A.

Project Personnel

CENTRAL STAFF

ASHMORE, HARRY S., Executive Editor, *The Arkansas Gazette*, Little Rock, Ark.

HAMMER, PHILIP G., Executive Officer, Committee of the South, Atlanta, Ga.

FLEMING, HAROLD C., Assistant Director, Southern Regional Council, Atlanta, Ga.

HILL, MOZELL C., Professor of Sociology, Atlanta University, Atlanta, Ga.

GRIFFIN, JOHN A., Director of Community Educational Service, Associate Professor of Sociology, Emory University, Ga.

MORTON, RUTH A., Field Secretary, Community Relations Program, American Friends Service Committee, Philadelphia, Pa.

FIELD STAFF

ABRAM, MORRIS B., Attorney, Atlanta, Ga.

ALBRIGHT, A. D., Associate Director, Cooperative Program in Educational Administration, George Peabody College for Teachers, Nashville, Tenn.

AMERMAN, HELEN E., Committee on Education, Training and Research in Race Relations, University of Chicago, Chicago, Ill.

CALHOUN, MALCOLM, Board of Church Extension, Presbyterian Church of the U. S., Atlanta, Ga.

CARMICHAEL, BENNIE E., George Peabody College for Teachers, Nashville, Tenn.

CHIVERS, CARRIE G., Department of Sociology, Morehouse College, Atlanta, Ga.

CHRISTENSEN, HAROLD T., Chairman of Sociology, Purdue University, Lafayette, Ind.

CULVER, DWIGHT W., Associate Professor of Sociology, Purdue University, Lafayette, Ind.

DAVIS, WYLIE H., Professor of Law, University of Arkansas, Fayetteville, Ark.

DOZIER, EDWARD P., Department of Anthropology, Northwestern University, Evanston, Ill.

DOZIER, MARIANNE, Department of Anthropology, Northwestern University, Evanston, Ill.

DREWRY, GALEN N., George Peabody College for Teachers, Nashville, Tenn.

GANDY, JOHN M., Welfare Council of Metropolitan Chicago, Chicago, Ill.

GUPTON, FRED W., George Peabody College for Teachers, Nashville, Tenn.

HAM, VIRGINIA H., School of Law, University of Arkansas, Fayetteville, Ark.

HOPE, JOHN M., II, Race Relations Department, American Missionary Association, Fisk University, Nashville, Tenn.

JOHNSON, BENTON, University of North Carolina, Chapel Hill, N. C.

JOHNSON, EARL S., Professor of the Social Sciences, University of Chicago, Chicago, Ill.

JOHNSON, GUY B., Professor of Sociology, University of North Carolina, Chapel Hill, N. C.

JOHNSON, LOIS E., Department of Sociology, Atlanta University, Atlanta, Ga.

KINCHELOE, JAMES B., George Peabody College for Teachers, Nashville, Tenn.

LEFLAR, ROBERT A., Dean of the Law School, University of Arkansas, Fayetteville, Ark.

LEWIS, HYLAN, Professor of Sociology, Atlanta University, Atlanta, Ga.

MACLACHLAN, JOHN M., Professor of Sociology, University of Florida, Gainesville, Fla.

MERRILL, EDWARD C., George Peabody College for Teachers, Nashville, Tenn.

MOORE, R. EDGAR, George Peabody College for Teachers, Nashville, Tenn.

MURPHY, EMMETT J., University of North Carolina, Chapel Hill, N. C.

ODUM, HOWARD W., Professor of Sociology, University of North Carolina, Chapel Hill, N. C.

O'CONNOR, JOHN J., Professor of Sociology, Georgetown University, Washington, D. C.

OSBORNE, IRENE, Washington Representative, Community Relations Program, American Friends Service Committee, Washington, D. C.

PELLEGRIN, ROLAND J., Department of Sociology, Louisiana State University, Baton Rouge, La.

PIERCE, TRUMAN M., Director, Southern States Cooperative Program in Educational Administration, George Peabody College for Teachers, Nashville, Tenn.

ROBINSON, GLEN E., George Peabody College for Teachers, Nashville, Tenn.

SUTTON, WILLIS A., JR., Department of Sociology, University of Kentucky, Lexington, Ky.

SWANSON, ERNST W., Professor of Economics, Emory University, Ga.

SWANSON, LOUIS, Director of In-Service Education, Chattanooga City Schools, Chattanooga, Tenn.

TREAT, KERN L., School of Law, University of Arkansas, Fayetteville, Ark.

TROTTER, AMOS C. F., Marlboro County Schools, Bennettsville, S. C.

VALIEN, BONITA H., Department of Social Sciences, Fisk University, Nashville, Tenn.

WILDER, OREN B., George Peabody College for Teachers, Nashville, Tenn.

WILLIAMS, ROBIN M., JR., Director, Social Science Research Center, Cornell University, Ithaca, New York.

YINGER, J. MILTON, Professor of Sociology, Oberlin College, Oberlin, Ohio.

Studies Made for the Project

SCHOOL COST STUDY—Ernst Swanson, Emory University.

BIBLIOGRAPHY DIGEST—Hylan Lewis and Associates, Atlanta University.

POPULATION STUDY—John Maclachlan, University of Florida.

HIGHER EDUCATION STUDY—Guy Johnson and Associates, University of North Carolina.

> "A Study of the Admission and Integration of Negro Students into Public Institutions of Higher Learning in the South," Guy Johnson.

PUBLIC SCHOOL STUDY—Truman Pierce and Associates, Southern States Cooperative Program in Educational Administration, George Peabody College for Teachers.

LEGAL STUDIES—Robert Leflar, Wylie Davis, and Associates, Law School, University of Arkansas, Morris Abram.

> "A Study of the Legal Aspects of Racial Segregation in the Public Schools," Robert Leflar and Wylie Davis.

> "A Memorandum Developing Two of the Several Possible Supreme Court Decisions which the United States Supreme Court Might Announce in the Five Common School Segregation Suits," Morris Abram.

PAROCHIAL AND SECTARIAN SCHOOL STUDIES—Malcolm Calhoun, Presbyterian Church of the U. S. and John O'Connor, Georgetown University.

"A Study of Racial Integration in Protestant Theological Seminaries," Malcolm Calhoun

"Catholic Educational Integration in Border and Southern States," John O'Connor.

FIELD STUDIES

"A Memorandum on Negro-white Integration in the Cincinnati Public Schools, 1953," J. Milton Yinger, Oberlin College.

"Analysis of Integration of the Public Schools in Indianapolis and in Six Other Communities," Harold Christensen and Dwight Culver, Purdue University.

"The Public School System of Washington, D. C.," Irene Osborne, American Friends Service Committee.

"Integration of Schools in Arizona and New Mexico," Edward and Marianne Dozier, Northwestern University.

"Report on Race Relations in the Chicago Public Schools, 1947-1952," Helen Amerman, University of Chicago.

"A Study of the Integration of the Public Schools of Cairo, Illinois," Bonita Valien, Fisk University, and Willis Sutton, University of Kentucky.

"Case Studies of School Integration in South Jersey," John Hope II, Fisk University.

"Memorandum on School Integration in Topeka, Kansas," Morris Abram, Attorney.

SPECIAL STUDIES

"The Nation and the Negro: Agenda for Integration," Howard W. Odum, University of North Carolina.

"Research Memorandum on Negro-white Interaction and the Problem of Desegregation," Robin Williams, Cornell University.

"A Summary of School Integration in the Urban Metropolitan Areas of the Non-South," Earl Johnson, University of Chicago.

Selected Readings and Source Materials

Bond, Horace Mann. *The Education of the Negro in the American Social Order.* New York: Prentice-Hall, 1934.

Brameld, Theodore. *Minority Problems in the Public Schools.* New York: Harper and Brothers, 1949.

Brownell, Herbert, Jr., U. S. Attorney General, *et al.,* "Supplemental Brief for the United States on Reargument" (*Amicus Curiae,* Supreme Court hearing on public school segregation cases December, 1953). Washington, D. C.: U. S. Government Printing Office, 1953.

Bustard, Joseph L. "Administrative Experiences of the New Jersey Division Against Discrimination," *Journal of Negro Education,* Vol. XVII, No. 1 (Winter 1948).

Chambers, M. M. *The Colleges and the Courts: 1946-1950.* New York: Columbia University Press, 1952.

Couch, W. T. *What the Negro Wants.* Chapel Hill: University of North Carolina Press, 1944.

Davie, M. R. *Negroes in American Society.* New York: McGraw-Hill, 1949.

Delano, W. "Grade School Segregation: The Latest Attack on Racial Discrimination," 61 *Yale Law Journal* (1952), 730-744.

Drake, St. Clair and Horace R. Cayton. *Black Metropolis.* New York: Harcourt, Brace and Co., 1945.

DuBois, W. E. B. *Black Reconstruction.* New York: Harcourt, Brace and Co., 1935.

Frank, John P. and Robert F. Munro. "Original Understanding of 'Equal Protection of the Laws,' " 50 *Columbia Law Review* (February 1950), 131.

Frazier, E. Franklin. *The Negro Family in the United States.* New York: The Dryden Press, 1948.

Guzman, Jessie P., *et al.*, eds. *The Negro Year Book.* New York: William H. Wise and Co., 1952.

Hesseltine, William B. *A History of the South, 1607-1936.* New York: Prentice-Hall, 1936.

Johnson, Charles S. *Education and the Cultural Crisis.* New York: Macmillan Co., 1951.

————. *Patterns of Negro Segregation.* New York: Harper and Brothers, 1943.

————. *Shadow of the Plantation.* Chicago: University of Chicago Press, 1934.

Journal of Negro Education, Vol. XVI, No. 3 (Summer 1947). (A state by state summary of educational facilities for Negroes in the Southeast.)

————, Vol. XVII, No. 3 (Summer 1948). ("Negro Higher and Professional Education in the United States")

————, Vol. XX, No. 3 (Summer 1951). ("The American Negro and Civil Rights in 1950")

————, Vol. XXI, No. 3 (Summer 1952). ("The Courts and Racial Integration in Education")

Konvitz, Milton R. *The Constitution and Civil Rights.* New York: Columbia University Press, 1946.

Landis, K. M. *Segregation in Washington.* Chicago: The National Committee on Segregation in the Nation's Capital, 1948.

McGranery, James P., Attorney General, *et al.* "Brief for the United States" (*Amicus Curiae*, Supreme Court hearing on public school segregation cases December 1952). Washington, D. C.: U. S. Government Printing Office, 1952.

Murray, Pauli, ed. *States' Laws on Race and Color.* Cincinnati: Woman's Division of Christian Service, The Methodist Church, 1951.

Odum, Howard W. *Race and Rumors of Race: Challenge to American Crisis.* Chapel Hill: The University of North Carolina Press, 1943.

————. *Southern Regions of the United States.* Chapel Hill: The University of North Carolina Press, 1936.

President's Commission on Higher Education. *Higher Education for American Democracy.* Washington: U. S. Government Printing Office, 1947.

President's Committee on Civil Rights. *To Secure These Rights.* Washington: U. S. Government Printing Office, 1947.

Ransmeier, Joseph S. "The Fourteenth Amendment and the 'Separate but Equal' Doctrine," 50 *Michigan Law Review* 203, (December 1951).

Simpson, George E. and J. Milton Yinger. *Racial and Cultural Minorities.* New York: Harper and Brothers, 1953.

Southern Regional Council. *Questions and Answers: The Schools and the Courts.* Atlanta, Ga., 1953.

Tipton, James H. *Community in Crisis.* New York: Columbia University Press, 1953.

U. S. Office of Education. *Biennial Survey of Education: Statistics of State School Systems.* Washington, D. C.: U. S. Government Printing Office, all years.

Vance, Rupert B. *Human Geography of the South.* Chapel Hill: University of North Carolina Press, 1932.

Warner, W. Lloyd, *et al. Who Shall Be Educated?* New York: Harper and Brothers, 1944.

Williams, Robin M., Jr. *The Reduction of Intergroup Tensions: A Survey of Research on Problems of Ethnic, Racial and Religious Group Relations.* New York: Social Science Research Council, 1947.

Woodward, C. Vann. *Origins of the New South, 1877-1913.* Baton Rouge: Louisiana State University Press, 1951.

Wright, Marion T. *The Education of Negroes in New Jersey.* New York: Teachers College, Columbia University, 1941.

Index

(The titles of Charts and Tables appear in italics.)